C000094954

Presenting with Super Confidence – 79 tips and tricks for New& Nervous Presenters

Never Suffer from Stage Fright or Presenting Nerves Again.

Your Audience Will Love You!

Ana Maria Gonzales

Table of Contents

Introduction

In almost every profession, presentation skills come as a staple prerequisite to advancing your career. However, most of those who are compelled to give a presentation gamble organically using their natural instincts, set of skills, and assumptions without being correctly taught how to present in front of an audience. Therefore, it is only expected that one ends up feeling disappointed with the outcome - which is either boring their audience into submission or missing out on the important messages they wanted to get across.

Many argue that 50% of any presentation's success depends on the audience's willingness to listen, which translates into how invested they are in what you are about to say or their level of awareness of the topic. But the truth is, the success of any presentation boils down to the presenter and their ability to make the presentation interesting, informative, and compelling. We have all witnessed at least one car crash in slow motion while attending a presentation when it was evident that the presenter hadn't prepared enough, and relied heavily on improvisation and the glamor of their slides. The way out, while redeemed simply in words, can be summarized into three aspects; acquiring the set of skills needed to captivate any audience to give a compelling presentation, scripting the presentation down to the minute, and finally, practicing until you are confident enough to step into the spotlight.

Presentation is no different from having a conversation with a group of people, and like any process of communication, it goes both ways. On one side, you are the sender, where your message relies on your ability as a speaker to articulate your thoughts in a clear and interesting frame, and on the receiving end are your audience, who would show their engagement through either responding verbally or by the mere insinuation of body language.

The good news is that presentation is regarded as a skill for a reason, a calming notion to assure you that mastering presentation skills can be acquired, developed, and improved. I've taught numerous teams of executives the fine art of presenting. I do really think it is an art when you are able to utilize all the tools in your magic box to transfer your ideas into a persuasive call-to-action your audience would be motivated to adopt, and that is everyone's ultimate goal. You want your voice to be heard, your thoughts translated into appropriate action, and your business endorsed. This is why presenting is an art that can be taught with the right material and a willing student.

I've very much enjoyed presenting in many countries throughout my career in many multinational companies and to different audiences from various professional backgrounds. Many people I've guided throughout my journey have told me how their lives have dramatically changed for the better once they'd honed their presentation skills. Their needs had been met as soon as they were able to cross that bridge to achieve a 'hard to win' sale, acquire a new contract, and beat hundreds of applicants in landing the job of their dreams.

There are many benefits to mastering presentation skills other than sharing information; actually enhancing this skill has multidimensional advantages for yourself, your business, and your team. For starters, on a personal level, knowing that you can address any audience and mold your presentation in a way that suits them so they can relate to your message would flare up your confidence level. You will learn how to manage your stress levels and curb your glossophobia (aka, fear of public speaking) in an effective way that you can use to your benefit. On the business level, according to billionaire Warren Buffet, presentation is the one skill that can boost your market appraisal by 50% and, therefore, your salary level. The reason behind this is the fact that a high-quality presentation translates into a captivating message that highlights the needs your audience would be prompted to recall to turn into a guaranteed sale.

With excellent presentation skills, you would give off the vibe of professionalism on another level where you know what you are talking about, you've got the right tools to convey the topic, and the vision encourages stakeholders to further invest in your ideas. That, alongside your business ethics, would allow you the capacity to building better and long-lasting customer relationships. It also holds great value for your interpersonal communication among teammates, as you would notice a lower staff turnover rate, all thanks to your ability to interact appropriately and address your internal issues in a fair and professional manner. Moreover, your team would gain a mass amount of motivation, knowing that their hard work is noticed and presented with finesse and competence.

There are two reasons why most people dread presenting; the fear of public speaking (glossophobia), which affects 75% of the human race, and what I like to call 'delivering insecurities,' where the presenter is not confident enough when delivering the message the right way.

Accumulating the necessary tools to ace public speaking does not only advance your career and differentiate you from others but can cut down possible losses as well. Statistics have shown that those who fear to present to a room earn 10% less than those who don't, and accordingly have 15% less chance of being promoted to a managerial position. And let's be honest, climbing up the corporate ladder is the aim second to entrepreneurship. This aim requires loads of presentations, and convincing ones at that, as many organizations require a presentation or two in the hiring process. So you need to be proficient if you want to get that role! In fact, all sales executives, or any executive for that matter, in most organizations, big or small, require a good command of presentation skills to be able to persuade senior decision-makers to close almost any deal.

But the one mistake most executives make is focusing more on the content rather than the delivery when it has now become a fact of life that the most powerful presentations rely only 7% on content but rests heavily with 38% on your tone, and 55% on nonverbal communication (your body language). So the critical factor here is how to deliver to reach your targeted end goal.

Throughout my experience, I personally had made some terrible, heart-stopping, mistakes when it came to delivering a captivating presentation! But now, you don't have to! After reading this book and practicing some of the examples (then practicing them AGAIN!), you'll be well on your way to give a memorable presentation and deliver your message to your audience! You'll quickly gain the confidence you yearn along with many beneficial tricks you can employ to up your game.

Yes, it's scary to start. As Dale Carnegie puts it, "There are always three speeches, for every one you actually gave. The one you practiced, the one you gave, and the one you wish you gave," but the more you practice, the more you'll feel a sense of achievement and accomplishment, which will lead you on to greater things. In years to come, you'll look back and realize this was one of the best decisions you have made to develop your skills and learn to present the right way from an accomplished professional confidently!

What this book promise is a practical step-by-step guide that is not overladen with anecdotes, but instead hands you the solutions you need in an easy to read format. There is no better time for you to get started. I'm waiting to teach you how to gain so much from this valuable skill! Don't you deserve to start now?

Chapter 1: Where Do I Start?

Many presenters fall in the trap of jump-starting their PowerPoint before crafting their speech first. That is a BIG MISTAKE! Just as much as dragging the task until a day or two before the talk's due date. Your slides are there to help guide your audience through your presentation. They serve the percentage of your attendees who are visual learners. That means, if you have the opportunity to project your presentation and yet you choose to rely solely on words, you'd be losing almost a third of your audience.

We've all encountered public speakers that don't use PowerPoint at all, like people who give TED talks and others who only read their slides word by word, losing all sense of what a presentation should offer. Those are two situations you need to stay miles away from. Instead, you need to know the logic behind utilizing a PowerPoint in the first place. In a clearer sense, visuals should not replace you as a speaker, nor should they overpower your words. Slide shows can be used to hook the core goal of your speech in your audience's minds and make your talk more interactive, understandable, and entertaining. They are the

TIP#5: If you opt to use any web-based slideshow, like Google Slides and Prezi, you need to check for Wi-Fi availability in your venue in advance.

It is advisable to stick to one theme that runs throughout your presentation from start to finish, and preferably juggle a maximum of 3 colors within your slides.

TIP#6: If you need more colors for your subtitles, you can always refer to different shades of those three colors to unify the feel of your slides and create harmony.

Of course, life would be much easier if you are presenting on behalf of a client, a corporation, or an organization where a consistent pre-designed slideshow is an integral part of their communication policy. But if not, revert to a simple and sleek template where your words, charts, and images would be the star of your slides.

The Content: Presentations allow you to use all types of content, from the text to images, videos, GIFs, and charts. However, those elements can be categorized into:

Text: gives you the opportunity to shuffle your main ideas into a more concise form. You wouldn't be able to type in any content if your speech wasn't fully crafted, because you need to identify which phrases to place in there and in which order. Inserting the text usually needs an outline where you can highlight the parts from your speech you need your audience to focus on and the parts, which require visuals to accentuate. As a second step, you need to work on your selection of words to phrase your ideas in a concise yet clear and simple way for your audience to understand.

TIP #7: Avoid using big melodramatic words in your presentation.

Keep it specific in simple terms that are easily understandable by all audiences. To do that, ask yourself: "If an undergraduate were present in the room, would they understand this terminology?"

TIP#8: Always explain the contractions and provide definitions for the terminology you are using, even if presenting to professionals.

You also need to avoid bulky paragraphs and readjust your content in bullet points or short phrases, which can guide your audience along with your presentation as well as serve as speaking cues in case you get distracted or forget what you need to say next.

TIP#9: Use the rule of 6! Include no more than six words per phrase and six lines per slide.

TIP#10: It's preferable to show one bullet point at a time to minimize audience distraction.

There are a couple of rules regarding how much you should write in each slide. In general, each slide should hold no more than one story, one category, or one subtitle. Remember that your slides should purpose of arranging your slideshow is to create a similar tingle to a compelling story that has a launch point, a peak, and a convincing closure. As you move from one slide to the next, the transition should feel smooth and easy. If not, then you need to revisit the slide order, or the content itself. But perhaps the most challenging factor faced by presenters is when their topic has no specific logical flow. There is no sequence for them to follow; for example, when presenting about "better managerial techniques," topics like these can be categorized into different management techniques and clusters, yet there won't be a right or wrong hierarchy to the slides. The way to cheat this kind of confusion is by following your instincts in regards to whichever organization feels more comfortable and natural to you as a presenter.

The Delivery: While everything looks good separately, the speech is well written and packed with credible data, and the slides seem neat and organized, you still need to tie those two elements together. And that is the fatal mistake most presenters make - they tend to overlook the final step, which is the delivery. How are you going to use your PowerPoint while on stage or in a meeting room while presenting? To achieve proper delivery, you need a bunch of 4x6 index cards and a copy of your speech with the slideshow open on your screen. First, start by numbering your index cards according to the numbering of your slides, and as you read the bullets, scrap down the part of your speech that you would like to communicate to your audience in your card and follow the same pattern until the very last slide. Then related to the previous history, similar cases, competitors, elusive findings, and relevant issues that might affect or be affected by your issue. You might not need all that additional information, but you'd be surprised at how much those extra bits could come in handy when you want to provide your audience with a real-life example or previous experiences. However, you don't need to stress yourself out too much about it. Just read to widen your horizons, and it's okay if you don't know everything that remotely relates to your subject. It's only necessary to know what you are talking about to the core. In fact, if your presentation allows for a Q&A or audience discussion and you come face to face with a baffling question that you don't have an answer to, you can always use the magic response: "*I'm not sure I have a solid answer for that at the moment, but I must thank you for sparking my curiosity to learn more about it. We are all learning, aren't we?*"

2. Research your Audience

At this point, you should at least be familiar with the nature of your audience to tailor the final adjustments of your presentation accordingly. For public talks, such as motivational speeches or life wellness symposiums, you might have no clue who will be walking in to listen to you speak in terms of background, age, or even gender. Make sure that you always refer to the organizers when wanting to know the estimated number of attendees.

However, things become much easier for tailored talks where you are going to present to a group of stakeholders, academics, or a group of enthusiasts. It is safe to say that presenting in front of an already established group of people who have a wide knowledge of your topic, can limit the content of your presentation to core information that they can build on. What can save you in this situation is knowing the purpose of your talk. Is it to inform them? Or is it to persuade them to close a deal or take a stance?

Whichever the case is, another aspect that can influence the presentation style is the session schedule, as the time of day can heavily influence the audience's reaction to your talk. Morning talks are considered the most productive as people are in their most alert state of mind, free from distractions because they haven't been crammed with tons of information. They will be in an interactive state, so you might like to make the best out of this through creating an interactive format where you can ask questions, or even call out some of the attendees for participation. You don't need to change the entire structure of the presentation but rather incorporate a few interactive elements here and there.

Things will start to slow down if the talk is scheduled in the afternoon after lunch, as people tend to get lethargic, so you might want to consider upping your game. It is advisable to shift the format of your presentation from a one-man show to an interactive workshop type. You can get them talking to each other or moving around and switching their seats if possible.

For example, you can instruct your audience to ask each other about something or shake hands. You can also insert a joke or two, but always make sure it's appropriate and non-offensive.

The second best time to give a presentation is in the evening when people come willing to listen and learn. Thus, there is a higher chance that you won't lose your audience, and they will be relatively focused as well. The tricky issue here, however, is that your audience will be the most critical to your content as they are there for a reason and by choice. So, if you don't deliver with quality and within the designated time, you will be showered with negative feedback.

3. Watch Professional Speakers

There is nothing wrong with finding inspiration from other presenters. This can help you structure both your presentation and your delivery in a more captivating way. You will find tons of speeches online that most probably address topics similar to yours. Take notes of the techniques used and pay close attention to their tone of voice and body language. But pay special attention to two things when selecting who to follow; first, the date of the speech - the more recent, the better because this means you can brush up on the latest tricks in presentation and audience interaction. Presentation skills are continuously evolving. There once was a time when using hand gestures was considered a sign of hesitance and a lack of confidence, while now it is regarded as an integral factor to get your message across to the audience.

Second is the source. Because the internet is an open and free space, anyone can post anything online, but you need to make sure that you are watching professional speakers from whom you can learn a thing or two.

4. Determine Your Presentation Style

Are you an enthusiast or a calm speaker? Do you like to use humor and sarcasm when possible, or are you straight-up serious? Do you prefer to address your audience with argumentative questions or just lay down the information in a logical sequence? Figuring out a style of presenting that you are comfortable with is directly proportional to your personality and your day-to-day interactions. If you pay close attention to how you speak in general, it can help you determine your natural pattern. Remember that when you're nervous, there is very little you can do to control your performance as your brain will focus on calming your nerves to prevent you from looking shaky and hesitant. Of course, as you gain more experience with presenting, you'll acquire the skill to shift from casual to professional and from calm to motivational depending on what emotions you want to channel to your audience. But, if this presentation is one of your earliest trials, it would be better to find a compromise that mixes your natural vibe with how you want the outcome to look.

5. Run through the Presentation

When you reach this point, there shouldn't be any significant edits left in your presentation, so you are ready for a test drive. The most important thing to control those confining jitters is to appear calm and confident. First, you need to know that it's completely normal to experience stage fright. It's ok to have sweaty palms and racing heartbeats that can be heard miles away. It happens to everyone; even the best speakers that the world has witnessed admitted the fear, including Mahatma Gandhi and Abraham Lincoln.

Moving forward, you need to prepare yourself mentally by knowing that your audience came to listen to you because you KNOW what you're talking about. They are not rooting for you to fail. On the contrary, they want you to succeed in giving them what they came for. A great piece of advice would be to mask your fear with excitement since both emotions are of high arousal in nature. Studies have shown that by admitting you're excited to your audience, you'll be perceived as more persuasive and proficient while delivering your speech.

Another effective piece of advice would be to learn your presentation visually. As human beings, we remember 10% of what we hear, 20% of what we read, but 80% of what we see and do. That's why it would be much easier to use signs, colors, or symbols and connect it to your presentation. By doing this, you will be fixating the information in your mind, so you don't have to awkwardly pause every now and then as you try to retrieve content. This step can be done on your personal note cards, which no one will see. You can use different highlighter colors, different bullet shapes for each point, and a mapped train of your presentation outline entailing where you begin and where you should wrap up for a final conclusion. Take note of colors and patterns that can help you remember significant insertions. For example, you can use a red circle for an example, a blue square for the main point, and a green triangle for sub-points.

6. Practice Out Loud

There are four ways whereby you can rehearse your presentation; you can step in front of a mirror with your laptop resting on a side table and note cards in hand. You can start presenting to yourself, but if this is your first attempt, it would be advisable to use it as a trial by breaking down the presentation into parts and articulating what you want to cover for each one. Memorize it and repeat until you are satisfied with the outcome before moving on to the next part.

Video recording is another option that you can rely on to critically review your body language, but it wouldn't be advisable to use this method if you are just starting to practice since it can make you feel discouraged. Both of the aforementioned ways would give you great insights into what you need to say and when to say it.

But the one thing that is overlooked is the fact that you will be presenting to an audience ... a live audience. So you need to know the level of the impact their presence would have on you. It's like taking it one step at a time and familiarizing yourself with the feeling of other people's presence as you speak. Accordingly, it's better to rehearse in front of a group of friends, honest and compassionate people who will offer you beneficial feedback on how to enhance the presentation. However, always practice on your own first until you are confident enough to take it to the more intimidating level of presenting in front of a group of familiar people, and later, to a group of strangers.

On a side note, be a selective listener when it comes to their advice and comments, meaning that you don't have to follow everyone's feedback down to the word, especially if it signals tearing the entire structure of your presentation down. Just choose what can add to your presentation in terms of making it more engaging and compelling.

Also, it helps significantly if you have multiple distractions around which can substitute for what you might experience if someone in the audience sneezes, moves around in their seat, stands up to leave, or a door opens and closes. Having loud music on, opening a window to the busy life of the streets, and allowing them to resonate in your room or a movie playing in the background can prepare you well. Being able to master presenting even when distracted helps you come across as a professional speaker. While it sounds minimal, the smallest distraction can cut your stream of thought, and you will end up stuttering as you try to refocus on what you were saying.

Another element you should pay close attention to is your body language and tone of voice. Remember that for your message to translate well to your audience; it relies 55% on your body language, 38% on your voice tone, and only 7% on your actual content. It's actually funny, considering the amount of time and effort spent on scripting the presentation while very little of both is spent on the two factors, which can make or break it. Maya Angelo said it best, "At the end of the day, people won't remember what you said or did; they will remember how you made them feel." And what better way to achieve that than playing with your tone of voice, where you can go deep and slow for emphasis, or high and fast-paced for excitement. You can employ pauses after an important statement to magnify its significance and use your hand gestures to lock in the concept. But, one thing you have to be aware of while rehearsing, is you need to make sure your body language isn't negating the message your words are trying to covey. One of the most popular examples is saying, "I'm very happy to be here with you today," while shaking your head from side to side instead of using the assuring head bob. You need to mind those minute details as well as your facial expressions to make sure you are not the one getting in the way of delivering an impactful presentation.

7. Time Your Presentation

If your talk is scheduled in between other speakers as part of a conference or an event, then you should know the time allocated to your participation. You need to time your presentation while keeping in mind that you need 10-15 minutes at the end of your talk for Q&A. But, if you're presenting to your team or stakeholders without an announced time frame, then break a 45-minute presentation into two parts where you can employ a breaker (a joke, quote, or a story) after the first 20 minutes, as most audiences tend to lose focus after that.

In order to perfect your timing, start with estimating how much time each part of your presentation would take. For instance, how much time do you need for the introduction? How much time would you need to explain a chart? And so on. After that, you can start practicing with a timer to enhance better your performance vs. the time allowed. Accordingly, make the necessary adjustments to fit in all the points you need to cover during the specified time. Beware of getting dragged into a story or bombarding a point with many examples; those are all-time crashers. Instead, stay focused, concise, interesting, and to the point, because the worst thing is over-running your time, especially if other speakers are scheduled after you. You'll find yourself in an unprofessional situation where you would need to wrap up abruptly without a proper closing.

8. Dress the Part

Whether you like to admit it or not, people tend to judge others by their looks long before you have the chance to utter a hello. They shape their first impression within 7 seconds! Other research findings have even concluded that within almost a tenth of second, vital traits such as trustworthiness are determined about you. The first impression happens only once, and so you need to start on the right foot to cross miles of having to position yourself as someone worthy of your audience's time. Therefore, you need to base this establishment by dressing the part, with the right attire and proper grooming.

As a fundamental rule, you should always look for comfort; comfort always channels confidence. But you don't want to dress too casually that you'd end up jeopardizing your status for someone who doesn't care or didn't try hard enough. This depends on the dress code provided by the organizers or your work attire policy if you are giving a routine internal presentation. You don't want to stand out as over-the-top, but attempt to mimic your audience by dressing as they do, if not a bit smarter.

For that to happen, it's important to know who your audience is. This could help you decide on what to wear. Whether they are young entrepreneurs, established businessmen/women, or a random group of people. It's definitely much easier if you're presenting to just one category, but if not, be equipped with a few accessories or additional garment pieces to decide whether to dress up or down. You need to also take into consideration the following demographics to suit up accordingly and avoid offending anyone:

- Gender

- Age

- Occupation

- Education

- Culture

- Religion

- Political Affiliations.

You can choose the silhouette by deciding on a blazer and matching pants, a full suit, or a loose shirt, that also depends on the presentation formality level. In all cases, make sure the clothes fit you perfectly, and nothing is oversized or too tight. All items should be perfectly pressed and clean, including your shoes. Don't go for a worn-out pair just because they're comfortable; it is always worth investing in new shoes that are just as comfortable. An important issue for women in heels. You want to look tall and sleek, but the long hours can be a killer in uncomfortable stilettos, and the click and clack against the floor can be heavily annoying when moving around.

When looking for the right clothes, there are a few helpful tips you can use to select your outfit with ease for your presentation. First, opt for dark-colored pants when possible. Colors like blue, black, and gray are great options for almost any occasion. If you're wearing a dress or skirt, make sure they're loose to allow for easy walking across the stage and make sure they're below the knee. Just make sure you're careful of your position on stage. If you're above the audience, that can be a bit embarrassing.

Go for a blouse or button-down dress shirt in a friendly and welcoming color. Pick out a pair of elegant shoes that are also comfortable. Remember that dark shoes go with most outfits. And when it comes to accessories, try to stick to some that are not too shiny or grab attention. They should add to the outfit, not distract your attendees.

The color selection matters to a great extent as well, where you have to put background colors into consideration. You don't want to blend into the extent that you appear like a floating head, and you don't want to heavily contrast with the background to the point that just looking your way would hurt the eyes. Instead, aim for a monochrome look that is easy and sophisticated. The psychology of colors plays a vital role here, where going for subtle tones makes you appear as someone who is approachable, while darker tones would place you in a more authoritative light.

The following tips will help you further with your choices:

• **Black:** is always associated with power, illustrating you as confident and stable. Nevertheless, it imposes a sense of authority. Overdoing it with black can turn the table on you. It might frame you as harsh and distant, so always add a hint of color to break the darkness.

• **White:** is associated with pureness. Too much might channel you as naïve and innocent. Mixing white with other pastel colors will portray you like sharp, clean, and established. On another note, it can make some skin tones look very pale. So be careful when going with this color.

- **Blue:** is a very common and safe color, especially for the darker tones which encompass more sophisticated shades, like navy. It gives a sense of serenity and accessibility. People who wear a lot of blue are perceived as credible, straightforward, and considerate.

- **Gray:** is a critical color that needs to be worn wisely. It all comes down to choosing the right shades while adding the right color hues to match. Again, as mentioned earlier, anything that's overdone can be a deal-breaker. With gray, you could look dull, boring, and unremarkable.

- **Green:** is a tricky choice because you can either look horrible or extremely classy. But it all depends on choosing the appropriate shade. It can support in a neutral look, but that would be established with, for example, a dark emerald green dress for ladies, or a blazer to pop some color in a monotone casual attire for men.

- **Red:** although a powerful color, can still be perceived as hostile, which is not something you would want to channel during your speech. Do not opt for a completely red outfit, but rather add an accessory that would add a catchy and elegant essence.

- **Yellow:** comes across as cheerful and bright.But it's not advisable to wear too much yellow during public speaking events as it can tire the eyes very quickly, thus losing the attendees' focus.

A trick you can use is to wear your full presentation outfit while rehearsing in the comfort of your own home. It gives you a better expectation for the movement you'd experience on stage and the sounds of your added accessories against the microphone. You don't want any juggles and jingles distracting your audience as you speak.

9. The Venue:

It makes a world of difference if you can have the chance to see the place where you'll be presenting before the actual day of your talk. It can drastically ease your mind if you have the chance to visualize the place as you are preparing for the presentation. But if you can't visit the venue due to your tight schedule or location, you can always ask the organizers about the size of the conference room and the seating arrangements to be able to determine the final format and plan for audience interaction. Knowing this kind of information, for example, will dictate whether you would need a microphone, for example, so everyone attending can hear you. You should also ask about the availability of a projector and the kind of equipment used to check for compatibility with your own laptop, and whether or not you'd need to purchase any cables to connect with your electronics. If all this information is unattainable, then it is advisable to arrive at least an hour earlier to familiarize yourself with the place and have a reasonable time to set up.

ANA MARIA GONZALES

Chapter 3 Technology will be the Death of Me!

Sometimes the unexpected happens, and you find yourself face to face with an audience 'naked' without a slide show, without an intriguing video, and nothing to share but your words and your presence. Many things can go wrong in the blink of an eye, and you need to prepare for when that happens. The utmost priority goes to backing up your work, whether it is your speech or your data. Always have it saved safely in cyberspace on your email and online drive for easy retrieval. In addition, have a copy of your essential material on a hard drive, may it be a USB or external hard drive, for when you experience an internet cut off.

We can't emphasize enough the importance of setting up for your presentation early. If that is not possible due to other speakers being on stage, then at least make sure that the organizers have tested everything out for you, including the sound equipment and the computer's vitality. It's also crucial to know the software, which the venue uses because you can't just expect Microsoft to work smoothly on a Macintosh, and vice versa. You also need to mind the file type of your PowerPoint and videos, so you won't be surprised on the day of your presentation that you are in need of converting software. Moreover, you absolutely must double-check the connecting cables from your laptop to the projector and have a spare of your own for any unexpected turn of events. All of this depends on whether or not the organization you are presenting at will allow you to use your own computer, especially places like security organizations, governmental entities, or defense contractors who won't allow any foreign technical pieces of equipment on their premises.

There are numerous scenarios for technology mishaps that would leave you baffled as you wrack your mind for other alternatives to keep the show running. Believe it or not, things like this happen all the time, no matter how much you prepare to avoid them. Sometimes technology runs its course! Even the most experienced speakers have been challenged by technology more often than not. But what differentiates a great presenter from an amateur one is their ability to turn any fail to their favor.

However, you must take care not to overcompensate the absence of technology by being too over the top with your voice and content. You don't want to be too calm either by merely standing there waiting for things to turn out for the better. First, you need to decide what to do with your audience during these times. It all comes down to you in terms of whether or not you will let your audience in on the problems arising, but we believe in turning lemons into lemonade and using that to your advantage by addressing the issue and mocking it. This strong command over the situation will assure your audience that they are in good hands with a professional speaker who owns other tools to present.

So what can go wrong?

A sudden power cut can ruin the ambiance while you are in the midst of your presentation. Hence, you need to make sure your laptop is fully charged, and you have a printed copy of your slides ready, so you can carry on with your mission. That is, of course, if the room doesn't go pitch black because of the lack of windows or an evening session. In that case, it would be the perfect time to insert a joke like, "*I don't know who prayed for that, but God was listening. Thankfully you can no longer see me, but, unfortunately, you can still hear me,*" while signaling your presence through making a knocking sound for your audience to look your way.

A temporary fail can also occur if the computer freezes or stubbornly refuses to project your PowerPoint onto the screen. It won't matter if you have your notes and presentation at hand. Other times, you'd be surprised by an inadequate microphone that won't work. That shouldn't be a problem if you are presenting in an office or a classroom. But what if you are presenting in a hall with over 100 people? Then you would have to step off the stage, move among your audience, and raise your voice.

It's also useful to download some applications on your phone to substitute for a clicker at times when the remote batteries decide to die on you. There are many easy-to-use Apps available such as SlideShow Remote, I-Clicker Remote, and Remote Mouse.

Let's just say that, as long as there is light in the room, there is no problem for you to go on. After all, people can hear you. If you manage to deliver meaningful content to your audience regardless of the tools you use, then your work here is done.

Now, what can you do instead?

While giving a presentation that employs audio, visual, and media is a powerful one, most professional speakers stress the importance of having a **plan B** for when things might go wrong. Those are things you can use to replace the presence of the visuals - which is your PowerPoint - the audio, which is your microphone, and the media, which includes a short clip or a video. The key here is how you shift the focus of your audience back to you, especially if there are people running up and down trying to figure out a solution to bring things back to normal. In the following bit, you will be presented with some of the most guaranteed techniques you can apply when technology fails you and your audience.

1. Using a Prop

A prop is any object that you can use to project a powerful metaphor and lock your audience in. Metaphors portrayed in a physical manner or even linked to an object they can see in front of them can help convey a high sense of emotions that are easily recalled.

In general, it is better to hold the object in your hands while you are talking about it rather than describing something invisible. That's why developers have 3D models available on display for their projects so clients can see something tangible. The thing about prop is that they aren't self-explanatory because they hold different meanings for every context, thus sparking everyone's curiosity to know how it can possibly relate to your talk. It can be anything from a chair to a single fruit, to a piece of garment, or even a simple cup. The whole point depends on how the prop relates to your talk, and it has to make sense!

Using a prop is much easier if you are discussing a humanitarian issue or calling for advocacy, but it presents a bit of a challenge for a business setting. In other words, what kind of prop can you use to grab your audience's attention while pitching an idea to stakeholders? There are numerous examples, but perhaps using a *lock* to signify your problem or the market gap you are addressing, and a *key* as your proposed business solution, can get the presentation rolling on the right note. Remember, you have 10 seconds to grab your audience's attention, so you better make it powerful.

2. Start with an Activity Followed by a Provocative Question

At a presentation about finding purpose in life, the speaker asked each person in the audience to scribble down six essential goals that they wake up to achieve every day. Then she asked them to rearrange these goals in ascending order from the most important to the least. After which she asked them to cross out one goal they could let go of and then another one and then another until each audience member was left with only one goal they felt the most passionate about. She requested that the audience circle that goal and write it in bold on a new empty paper. Then she said, "*There you have it, laying right in front of you in bold - your ultimate life goal. Now answer this, are you willing to dedicate your entire life to materializing that goal?*!"

And just like that, the audience is instantly enticed as they knew what she was talking about instead of listening to an entire speech about something that is vague and undefined in their minds. This technique helps engage your audience, get them thinking, and encourage them to follow the train of thought as they are now a part of it.

3. Engage with a Story

Many speakers can't get enough of using stories to anchor the core message and persuade their audience to take the action they are after. Stories, better known as narratives, are the earliest form of teaching known to mankind. They are used as a powerful tool that can be used to pass along a valuable message while packaged in an entertaining and easy to follow scenario. It also presents a great substitution for when technology fails, and you need to maintain your audience's attention.

In the business world, using narratives seems to be a frowned-upon approach. To the corporate world, it feels like it's less professional if data isn't presented in charts or bullets while there is nothing wrong with cutting to the chase with straight-to-the-point information, more times than not you will need to tap into the audience's emotions to motivate them to endorse your business.

Storytelling's powerful effect stems from the art of persuasion, which we discussed earlier in chapter one because it helps bring the audience on board with you along with a journey to a final destination you want them to reach. It doesn't matter if you are a startup business pitching for investment, or if you're a sales manager presenting to potential buyers or to your superiors. If you manage to paint a picture, humanize matters, and evoke emotions through narrative, you will be able to motivate and persuade your audience in just a matter of minutes.

If you think about charities, for example, whose sole purpose is to raise money for a cause, they always ditch the numbers and adopt storytelling instead in their advertisements, email marketing, and social media platforms. This is because they know that for them to guide people to their call-to-action, they need to involve them emotionally. You'll come across thousands of heartbreaking stories about abandoned children, endangered species, and homeless people, and you'd feel the compassion and urge to do something about it. The list is endless when it comes to stories that carved their effects on the hearts of advocates and donors.

This can also be applied to any business sector where the audience wants to hear about the struggles and challenges that you had to walk proudly through to get where you are today. They want to learn about the hefty impact of an issue on your business development and how much of a relief it would be to cross that bridge to a brighter perspective.

4. Generate a Laugh

Laughter triggers the release of dopamine in the human body, which is what scientists call "the happy hormone." Your aim is to be remembered, and what better way than making your audience laugh? However, many speakers argue the fact that they are not 'naturally funny' or don't possess the right skills to make people laugh - but that is not the point. You don't have to narrate a situation for people to laugh. On the contrary, in this case, less is more. You can search for funny jokes online that are appropriate and free from offensive insinuations. You can always apply the magical effect of a long pause accompanied by an eyebrow raise and a head tilt after proposing a situation. And you can mention a funny part from a movie or a TV show that relates to your topic. Sometimes speakers like to use political decisions as a metaphor for channeling their message. But, if power and technology are up and running, then you can rest easy, knowing that showing a funny clip or assigning a funny GIF as your backdrop while narrating a situation will drag laughter out of your audience.

Chapter 4: Okay! You're Going on Stage!

It takes a lot of courage to overcome all the nervousness that goes hand in hand with going on stage, but remember that you are there for a higher purpose: Adding to people's knowledge. Besides, this won't be the last time you get anxious about going on stage. This will happen again and again, no matter how many times you present. The only difference is that the impact of those jitters will definitely lessen, until one day, they're the exciting little nerves that pump you up before you step out in front of the audience.

Think carefully about how you want the beginning of your speech to influence your audience. You can do so by asking yourself the following questions, and the answers should guide you to the best approach.

- *What is the first thing I want them to experience?*

- *What kind of first impression do I want to project to them?*

- *What kind of emotions will my introduction evoke in the audience?*

Remember, what you say isn't the only aspect that creates an impression. The room you're presenting in, the lighting, the biography printed in the outline manual, the pre-presentation images on the projector or a video of your previous speeches, how you're dressed, your posture, how you enter the room and whether you present yourself or if someone else is presenting you. All of these factors come together to contribute to shaping your audience's first impression of you.

In addition to that, providing an enticing introduction is essential to set the tone of your presentation and ensure that the message and energy you want to channel are directly communicated to your audience.

The time has come for you to present all the content you've crafted, and the delivery means you've practiced. So, let's get this show started.

Think about your Opener Options

Usually, the first 2-5 minutes of presenting yourself and your ideas are the most influential. The first few words always determine if you've captured the audience's attention or not. Choosing the right words to describe who you are and delivering it with authenticity is what will keep them hooked for the rest of the presentation.

While introducing yourself, try being more open to adopting new creative ideas rather than the traditional means of listing all your credentials and professional achievements. Instead, you can first try to break the ice with welcoming your audience instantly, asking how they're feeling and whether or not they are excited to be there to hear what you have to say. Remember that presentations, no matter how serious they are, should be entertaining. Not necessarily shallowly entertaining or cheesy, but packaged in an attractive yet informative format.

You can utilize the opportunity to make them laugh and create a more laid back atmosphere. Using humor is effective when trying to persuade people and even more powerful when trying to create a connection with them. A very common example for a simple opening laugh is to say sarcastically, "Well, if you thought that you're here today to know more about (insert your topic), you're wrong!" This will instantly grab their attention, stir a bit of laughter, and will give them the impression that you are a more approachable person. After that, you can readjust the statement by sharing with them your through-line, the core message of your speech. Another option if you are addressing a humanitarian issue is to start with, "The world is a bad place, right? And I'm here today to show you just how darker things can get!" And follow that with "Just Kidding, I'm here today to showcase the problem and try, together, to find a better solution." But bear in mind that humor must be used carefully, since too much of it can seem unprofessional.

While scanning the room, you must try to determine the approximate age of your audience, keeping in mind what would catch their attention, and what would be commonly relevant to all of them. Thus, if you feel that your audience won't appreciate jokes, then don't attempt it. Always be prepared with a real-life story or case study to share instead.

Maintaining eye contact with your audience also establishes a link or bond that keeps them connected and focused on what you are saying. Not only that, but it will give them a chance to respond and be active. This will definitely shift your passive listeners to active members, participating and engaging in your topic with an eagerness to hear what you have to share. Always seek out the 'nodders' among the audience to serve as a barometer, giving you an indicator of how well everyone in the room is receiving your delivery.

Be Succinct

The audience's attention is what you are trying to gain. After all, getting the attendees hooked and keeping them interested for as long as you can, should be your top priority, while at the same time trying to convey your message in a simple and concise way. This can be done by fragmenting your speech into smaller chunks and giving life to your words with precise and colorful language.

Presentation skills demand a lot from the speaker, so using familiar and easily comprehensible words could help you cut to the chase, since they are understood easily and immediately. Choose words that most accurately depict what you want to convey. As human beings, we all have the capacity to accept and perceive new information. Yet, most concentrate for approximately 20 minutes before they lose interest and begin to disconnect. Don't add to their misery by using complicated language. While presenting, it's not the best time to show off your extensive vocabulary. Remember, it's about your audience, not you. You definitely don't want them to end up busying themselves with checking their phones for synonyms and getting distracted or bored just because they can't understand you.

So focus on delivering your ideas and shifting from one point to another smoothly in a simple and constructive way by using easy sentences. The last thing you want is to confuse your audience because you can't link part of your speech to the next. You must know your script by heart and ensure that your entire presentation focuses on just that.

Keep your points specific to try to eliminate any broad and unnecessary topics. Remember, your time is limited and you need to deliver all your points within the allotted time. Always keep in mind that sharing stories or delivering a point through stories or comparing situations, especially when explaining complex ideas, are not a waste of time if chosen and placed wisely. It can be effective because the use of ideas, information, and statistics can help keep your audience refreshed when you elaborate on your topic using a different structure.

It helps if you mind the significance of your main topics and occasionally repeat the main message in different words to keep your audience interested and in sync with what you are doing. You can simply say, *"Another important aspect of (insert your main topic) is..."* Or *"One of the most important things you need to know about (insert your main topic) is ..."* You can do this as many times as you like, but beware of sounding too redundant.

However, if you find yourself giving out too much information, you might need to reconsider the following reasons as to why you tend to overshare!

Positive reasons:

You are enthusiastic and want to share as much as possible about your topic with the audience. You can solve this dilemma by sharing a small booklet that has all the extra information you wish to share.

Negative reasons:

• You have been advised to fill up a certain time slot and weren't given enough time to prepare or rehearse.

• You haven't taken the needed time to sort out your talk and structure it properly.

• You were asked to include all the information, whether you like it or not, which means messing up the presentation you've prepared

• You are afraid of not being perceived as informed or knowledgeable enough and thought that by adding more information, it would help the situation. But adding more information might backfire and bore your attendees, so be careful of what you try to add.

Be Flexible

When you are forced to change your presentation according to changes in the time slot you are allowed, there are still a few tricks that you can use to help keep your presentation free from clutter and too much unnecessary information.

1. Preparing multiple versions of your presentation or your speech

You should have at least 3 versions of a speech as you practice! There is the 40-second version, where you can summarize the main headlines you are going to discuss. A 2 minutes version, where you elaborate on the importance of each headline in a maximum of two lines for each. And finally, the last version, which is the full version of the speech. The one, which you'll actually get to deliver. This method allows you to expand or contract the amount of detail they wish to include within each point, based on their level of importance to that particular audience.

2. Never let timing change the message

What matters the most is not to allow time constraints to take away from the main message you're trying to get across. It's okay if the level of detail you are able to dedicate to each point changes depending on how your audience reacts to each point, as well. But it's important not to sacrifice any important elements of your presentation to save up on the time factor.

3. Be prepared to go off track

Unscripted public speakers, those who rely on an outline and leave the rest to improvisation, are able to adjust the amount of time they spend on each individual point and adjust their topics to the given time slot they are allowed. They use their audience as their indicator for when they need to move on to the next point or elaborate more on the current one. To achieve that, use eye contact, look around the room, and analyze whether or not your words are being understood and perceived clearly. If you see hints of confusion drawn on your audience's faces, be smart enough to pick up on that and ask if there is more clarification required or if you need to provide further explanation on the topic.

4. Shuffle your content around

Remember that your audience hasn't seen the actual plan you've worked on for hours. So you are free to roam around the content while tailoring it to your audience's needs. You need to be able to sense your audience's boredom or pick up on distractions. If you encounter that, then it's time to be more engaging; use a story, a provocative question, a joke, or an image. You can employ any of the aforementioned techniques until you are reassured that you've drawn your audience in again before moving on to another serious point.

Do not get caught in a lie!

Sometimes, the pressure of being on stage and the desire to astonish and impress might force you to improvise. And most times, these elaborations will lead to a blown out of proportion 'lie.' It will be easy to spot, especially if you are 'on stage.' Whenever you come face to face with this situation, there are a few things that can be done to help you get things back on track and save your credibility and reputation.

• Own up to it

If you get caught, the last thing you should be thinking of is denying what you said, regardless of how tempting it may feel. Lying to cover up a lie is never a good idea. Avoid the temptation of using excuses and all sorts of justifications. Own up to it and admit you were wrong, and apologize sincerely for the dishonesty. After all, apologizing for any mistake shows character and integrity.

• Turn Things Around

Whatever you do, don't become defensive, even after your audience has discovered your lie. Use the lie as a chance to break the barriers by opening up a discussion. For example, reflect on the reasons why someone might feel the need to lie. Or maybe spark up a conversation about plagiarism.

• Never Again!

When the storm passes - and it will! - Make a promise to yourself that this will never happen again. You will never be caught in a lie by your audience. Instead, you'll do a better job of delivering what is expected from you.

• Learn and Move On

We all lie at some point. That's not a justification but more of a calming phrase to let you know that it happens to everyone. Usually, we lie to fulfill a neglected need. You need to analyze at what point during your presentation did you feel the need to lie and about what. Does it have to do with achievements? Recognition? Procrastination? Past experiences? A personal quality? Then you might have to consider finding a solution to turn that lie around. Do you need to work harder? Learn more? Talk to your superiors about being demotivated? Only you can recognize your low points so you can start improving.

Now that you've done all the preparation, turn your nervous demeanor into a passion!

Besides having well-rounded and deep content, professionally well-designed and planned visuals, and catchy props (if needed), it is all for nothing if you do not have deep, heartfelt confidence in your material. Be passionate about your topic and let that enthusiasm show and channel to your audience.

Here are some of the many tips that can help you get over your anxiety and straight into the presentation, thus averting the tendency of experiencing a panic attack.

• Getting straight to the topic without wasting too much time mumbling about random topics. In the beginning, stick to sharing the true purpose of why you are there.

• Be prepared for any issue that may arise and plan alternatives to control them.

• Focus all your energy on staying calm no matter what might happen, and remember to breathe.

• Ignore your inner thoughts, which might affect your confidence or that, might initiate a wave of self-doubt.

• Focus on your strengths, the fact that you have what it takes to present anything with passion and excitement, in order to transfer your emotions and enthusiasm to your audience.

• Rehearse several times and record yourself to analyze if there are any parts that you might need to change in your outline or delivery.

• Step in with confidence and a warm and welcoming smile. It's all going to be okay!

Finally, here is an easy to use checklist that you can implement after you have done all your

preparations to ensure that you are fully ready to take the stage.

1. I have rehearsed my speech enough times that I now feel comfortable

2. I have checked that my speech sticks to the time allotted, and there is enough room for a discussion.

3. I have recorded and/or videotaped myself and listened/watched it.

4. I have prepared my note cards and numbered them in case they get mixed up.

5. I have practiced pacing my breathing and noted the parts of my presentation, where I get too excited or anxious.

6. I have prepared all the visual aids that I may need, and I have checked the software compatibility.

7. I have saved my slides on an external drive and hard drive, and I have a soft copy on my email.

8. I have printed out my slides.

9. I have prepared all handouts that I wish for my attendees to have (optional).

10. I have proofread my speech and the slides word for word.

Chapter 5: Win with Rapport!

So the day has finally come! You are all set and equipped with the right resources and content. The crowd and setup might make you feel a bit overwhelmed and tense, and that needs to be set aside. You don't need to fixate so much on the jitters to get the show rolling. Instead, you need to boost your confidence and take control of the scene, and in order to get there, you should build rapport with your audience for the day.

A lot can be done to build rapport, starting from the moment you set foot in the venue until the very end of your speech. The following guide will help you get started with what to wear, meeting and greeting the audience, maximizing the benefit of presented content, the way you speak and deliver, and so much more. So don't worry, we've got your back! Just sit back and let us take you through the simple tips you need to win with rapport!

1. **How you look matters**

The way you look is as essential as the content is. One of the most important elements on your to-do list when preparing for the big presentation day is how you dress. Do not underestimate this aspect, as it plays a vital role in establishing rapport in terms of anchoring trust and showing leadership. For additional details, you can refer back to chapter 2, but as an initial thought, think about resembling your audience when the setting is suitable, to avoid the egoistic feel that might transfer to them. You are already on stage; you don't need to add more to that!

Deciding on what you'll wear depends on the theme and the audience you will present to. Let's say you're doing a Ted talk like a CEO of some major company. You need to suit up to reflect the culture of the workplace or the designation you bare. On the other hand, if you're a marketer presenting a plan to management, you would stick to the daily wardrobe you usually go with, but with a bit of smartness, rather than mere casual. This helps paint the picture of you in your daily setting but with an added professional look and feel to deliver your confidence and expertise in terms of what you are about to present.

We all remember the great Steve Jobs and how he set a memorable example in being efficient with his unified wardrobe choice in any public event. However, that does not mean you need to buy a dozen of the same exact shirt or pants to wear for each event. But you can apply the same concept through "branding" yourself with a certain style that is versatile enough to suit all events.

2. **Loosen up and meet the public**

This all depends on the time you have on hand before the actual presentation, type of event, and venue setting. Again, shrug that burden off your shoulders, since each and every setting has its tactics.

In case the presentation is informative, inspirational, or educational, and it's not so hard to point out your audience, go around, introduce yourself, and get to know them. Once communication is established, try to understand why they are attending the session, and what they are expecting to learn or get out of your talk. Make the most out of this connection, and link with them by placing yourself in their shoes, literally!

Ask yourself this. *If you were one of the audience members, what would you like to know?*

Doing this will provide space for you to craft your content accordingly, getting closer to their wants rather than just bombarding them with loads of information that won't be well-received from their end.

On the other hand, if it's more of a business presentation, with a product or service that needs to be endorsed, roam around smoothly among competitors and business peers aiming to understand what should be done to ensure a win. Remember that by avoiding what might go wrong, you'll have a higher chance of closing the deal. Make sure to be as smooth as possible while doing so. At the end of the day, business is all about competition, so sacred information won't be passed on straight away. This will certainly save you from falling into mundanely listing your product or service features with no intention to persuade. Instead, aim to guide your talk to tackle the aspects differentiating you from your competitors while catering to your customers' aspirations.

However, when you have no time to spare for social exchanges, several things could be done. The most common of all is shaking hands with the crowd and greeting them while they gather in place. This simple move breaks down a bit of the tension, thus paving the way for a more comfortable setting. They would feel welcomed, which might even enhance their interest, and they will listen and grasp the information a bit better than expected.

Last but not least, you can always invest in your opening speech to establish rapport. The initial words are as crucial as the main content. You want to build credibility and show good command of your topic if your audience is to trust you. But most importantly, the audience needs to feel they are in good hands, listening to someone who knows what they are talking about so they can be motivated to pay attention and learn. You can create an engaging opening that will grab their attention and instantly set them in the mood by sharing a story, providing real-life examples, or if you are capable of using humor, a witty joke!

3. **Emotional connection:**

Presenting formally in a professional manner does not mean setting emotions aside. It doesn't have to be cold, hard to relate to, and downright boring. The audience is sitting there thriving to acquire information from you, and for that to happen, a bit of empathy should be projected. To achieve empathy is to tap into the emotional elements of a story. And remember that everything has a story behind its existence. People love to hear about the struggles as much as the blessings, the failures as much as the successes, and all the emotional turmoil experienced. Even if you're pitching a product or service that you want your audience to buy, you can address the compelling reason behind providing it, why it was created in the first place, and how it can add value to their lives. The reason for this is that people buy with emotions justified by logic, not the other way around!

Accordingly, building an emotional connection is not about refraining from your professional look and feel, but rather attracting them to the topic from various real-life angles so they can relate and build on it. They need to be engaged and attracted to the material. Even if it's in a lecture, make sure to clarify that communication is always a two-way street that allows room for their interactions and comments.

On another note, to avoid making it all about the information, don't over-do it in an attempt to impress. Instead, prepare yourself mentally that today is not about you or what you have achieved, but rather about them and what they aspire to hear and grasp. Have them understand that you are here for them and that your sole purpose is sharing knowledge. You can achieve that by incorporating the three magical words every professional salesperson uses by saying something like this, "*I am here today to share with <u>you</u> the <u>new</u> <u>secrets</u> of making it big in the ultra-competitive digital marketing world.*" Using these phrases communicates that you are not here to showcase your expertise but rather for their benefit, which shows value. Using words like 'new' sets you apart from other speakers and makes it feel like you are providing something that they haven't heard before. And 'secret,' which will instantly spark the curiosity of your audience to listen carefully.

4. Simple and convincing

Simplicity can take the edge off of how heavy your content is, especially if you are discussing an already complicated topic. Make it simple by using well-structured short phrases. Simplify your terminology but within a limit as to not throw off the meaning. But make sure that by simplifying things, you are not affecting the value of your content to the point that it's too weak and shallow. Of course, this all depends on the audience's background; basically, you can level up or down if you know who you are presenting to. For example, presenting to a group of professionals can help you skip all the additional explanations you would have to provide if you were to present to an audience that is not familiar with your topic. But if you don't exactly know who you are addressing, make it a mix of both; explain more whenever needed, not with each uttered word that might or might not be a bit ambiguous.

Clarifying at the right time and refraining from maximizing it is a skill that can enhance audience persuasion. It is always true that when people are convinced, they are ready to listen more, especially when trust is developed.

5. Sway with your Voice & Tone

Another important set of elements that need emphasis and are the root of common mistakes across various presentations are voice and tone. Never underestimate the way you speak to your audience. It sets the energy level in the room, the attention span of the people, and the overall ambiance of the talk.

In general, always use a louder tone than usual, but not too loud that it gets overwhelming or intimidating. The higher-pitched notes are essential at the beginning to encourage concentration and alertness and are also necessary when making a point. After setting the high notes, it is also crucial to detect when you need to lower your voice. Lower notes make the audience feel at ease and connected with your talk on a subconscious level. Nevertheless, lower tones relay that you're relaxed and not nervous at all (even if you are). Tone variations enhance the concentration span of the audience, keeping them interested most of the time.

It's not only about setting tones, but rather your overall speech skills. You need to be aware of how to employ the powerful effect of the 'pause,' which you can use after making a point, ending a certain part of your topic, or just halting to give the people a chance to take in the information. It basically sets the proper mood for the audience to relax as well. But beware of overdoing it as it might send a message that the speech is over at some point. And if prolonged, people will start losing focus and interest.

Another element in regards to voice is pace, talking too fast, or too slow. It has to be maintained somewhere in the middle. Speaking very fast might sound as if you're very anxious, as opposed to slowing down the pace, which might give off the feeling that you have lost your train of thought.

We have mentioned a few pointers in building trust and authority earlier, but there is a small and significant issue that we all sometimes face, which is using a lot of "Um's" and "Ah's." Try to minimize those as much as possible - instead, just pause, minimally. Repetitions used to stop or recall might send the wrong message, making you look like you are not confident or thoroughly in command of your topic.

6. Watch and let them see *YOU*

After taking you through voice and tone, another element that can complete the picture of a solid professional speech is eye contact.

Eye contact is not just limited to looking the audience straight in the eye, but it is one of the essential elements that add volumes to your presentation along with the right body language. It can be used to initially deliver a message and exclude any intimidation, of course, depending on how you look at the audience. There are a lot of theories regarding the right and wrong ways of using proper eye contact. Here are two ways you can use eye contact to build rapport:

1. Focus on one person in the audience for five to seven seconds and then move quickly to another person on the opposite side of the room to spread the gaze. You may be wondering why five to seven seconds. Usually, this is the time it takes to finish a sentence and make a point.

Also, do not get hung up on actually counting the seconds in your heard. To avoid getting tense or overwhelmed, just make it smooth and random by somehow moving at more or less similar intervals.

2. Another way is to divide the room into parts. This method ensures you are making eye contact with as many people as possible. It also helps you avoid getting fixated on only one side of the room. This varies, of course, according to the venue.

A. *Large Halls:* This can be a large hall. Try to divide the room into six parts, where each side (right, center, and left) is further divided into two parts. This helps spread your eye contact equally. Mix and match your eye movement to enhance the rapport you're trying to build with the audience.

B. *Keynote speeches/ Small Halls:* This is a room with a center aisle and seats on each side. Basically, divide it into four parts and apply the same methodology of eye movement we've outlined above.

C. *Meeting/conference rooms:* These rooms usually cater to 40 people or less. In this case, how you divide the room depends on what makes you comfortable and gives you the ability to maximize eye contact.

All of these exercises enhance your eye contact with the audience, keeping you in control when looking at everyone, making each and every person in the room feel equally important and appreciated throughout the entirety of the presentation. Again, this taps into the emotional connection detailed earlier, and how important it is to engage your spectators.

7. **Flexible Content**

Your content or presentation is your framework. You should cover all aspects of the topic, but that does not mean that you should recite it exactly as it is written. You don't have to go at it word for word. Instead. As long as you convey the message in a clear way, it really doesn't make much of a difference. You might feel frustrated if you don't practice exactly what you rehearsed but bear in mind that your audience wasn't there during your practice sessions. Just let your stream of thought take over and color your speech with examples, and tell relatable stories that can be intriguing.

It's crucial to remember that prepared content is not your only purpose, but rather the roadmap that carries you through the speech and illustrates how flexible you can be to add to the content and maximize the audience's benefit. These aspects deliver on your poise and credibility, and in turn, make the audience trust you even more by enlightening them with your capabilities. You set your worth and boost the energy levels among the people, making them connect with you even more.

8. Manage Audience Expectations

One of the major rapport breakdowns is when you present something, and unfortunately, the audience is expecting something else. This can be in the form of an off-topic delivery, or missing out on some points that the audience was waiting for. To avoid this, always lay out the topics you want to cover during the speech upfront in order to frame their expectations. This way, they will eventually visualize what they are getting and capitalize on as much as possible. In a clearer sense, tell them what you are going to talk about. And of course, if you are one of the speakers at a big conference, your presentation topic should have been provided to the audience by the organizers days and maybe even weeks in advance.

Also, you need to relay how you would like the talk to go. Will you allow comments and questions during the presentation? Will you spare 15 minutes at the end of your talk for Q&A? Or, if that's not possible, will you meet them afterward or provide your contacts for further inquiries? All of this needs to be established so that your audience can be a part of your outline rather than just on the receiving end of it. Therefore, it's advisable to time your speech so that it takes no more than 80% of the time allocated to give room for questions or remarkable additions that can enrich your topic regardless of how informative it is.

Chapter 6: Compelling Information in a Concise Manner

This is where impact meets time! It's a fact that if you want to evoke change in just about anything, you need time. And a lot of time, at that. Actually, the statistics vary between 90 days all the way to an average of 2 to 3 years just for a change to happen and be retained! And no, we're not exaggerating. According to experts, this is how long it takes to impose a change in people's attitudes towards an issue. However, in presentations, you need to do just about that, but within a span of 20 -45 minutes!

So the question is, how can you go about doing that?

There is a quantitative surveying technique used to measure a change in perspectives that you can put to good use when crafting your content. That is the KAP, short for Knowledge; Attitude; Practice. In brief, the main idea is to test people's knowledge about an issue, assess their stance (for or against) the issue, and how a stance like this reflects on their actions. For you to affect and persuade your audience, any audience for that matter, to adopt a concept, a service, a product, or an advocacy issue, you need to cover three aspects;

1. Increase their awareness level and knowledge in regards to the topic you're addressing.

2. Persuade a change in their attitude by giving them all the compelling reasons why they should support or reject a notion.

3. And provide some sort of a guideline or road map they can follow to translate a change of attitude into action.

Bear in mind that there is a huge difference between a speaker who is there to influence through motivation and encouragement and one who is there to guilt-trip the audience and establish authority. The first uses the presentation to invite the audience to feel, then think, and then take action (in that precise manner), while the other jumps into the call-to-action without laying a solid foundation first. In other words, an impactful speech needs to speak to the audience in more ways than just awakening their critical thinking abilities.

So, how can you apply the same concept but stretch it along your allotted presentation time?

Let me break this chapter down into two crucial parts that are needed to deliver a compelling presentation in a precise manner;

First, let's tap into the many techniques you can use to craft an impactful message.

There are six fundamental E's you need to incorporate in your speech to be perceived as impactful by your audience:

1. **Educate** your audience by providing valuable and deep information about your topic. The aim is to increase their knowledge about the ups and downs of an issue, the reasons, the challenges, and areas of improvement. Remember that knowledge is key as it represents the foundation on which you can relay any call-to-action. Because the rule remains the same: When you know better, you do better.

2. **Entertain**, and keep the overall mode of your talk simple. Even if the topic is dense and the information you'd like to communicate is a real head-scratcher, that doesn't mean you have to enlist the facts and information in a boring way. People tend to learn more effectively when it's entertaining, not forced. So, you need to spend some time thinking about how you can package it creatively to make it less intimidating and hard to follow. The most effective technique of all is weaving the most tedious information into a story, or a timeline sequence of events. You can also utilize visuals, whether it's in the form of images or charts, to get your message across faster and with ease.

3. **Experience** through engaging your audience. Take them along the journey of your presentation as active participants rather than passive. However, this doesn't necessarily invite the use of hands-on activities, especially if the audience number is too large to manage. You can engage them on another level by

tapping into their other senses while narrating a story or describing a situation. The more they interact with your words, the more they relate to what you are talking about, and the more they'll retain the new information you've thrown their way.

4. **Excite** your audience through variations in your tone of voice and the right body language. Take them to an elevated altitude with a high tone and fast pace, conveying excitement and passion. And drag them down with a low voice and slow pace for emphasis or when projecting deep and dark emotions. These variations channel your message in a deeper sense that will surely radiate across the room. But mind your body language, and maintain one that is open with a straight posture and a high head for positive points, and slouch down to a closed-form with your shoulders, tilted head, and a hint of a hunched back to channel disappointment or sadness.

5. Use **examples** that the audience can relate to. Now, your examples shouldn't necessarily be limited to explanatory ones. In fact, it always makes a huge impact if you employ real-life examples with vivid details. And better yet, use your experiences or life's journey as one. Remember that, whether you like it or not, by being on stage, you are their best example. And by using a personal story, that is, of course, relevant to the topic at hand, you are connecting with your audience and effective building rapport.

6. **Encourage** through using positive psychology. More often than not, people tend to confuse

encouragement for intrusiveness, while it can be attained easily if people know what they need to do to bring about a change. There are many ways you can guide your audience subtly to a call-to-action. For example, you can draw the road map to what they need to do, learn, or change to achieve the desired outcome. You can reflect on yourself, saying. *"I've done it, and so can you."* And you can reflect on how your proposed call-to-action can be salvation from their crippling problems through painting a picture of how the grass would be greener once they endorse the change.

Another effective means to deliver a compelling presentation is through tapping into your audience's five senses. It makes a world of difference if your audience leaves your presentation, calling it an experience instead of a lecture packed with redundantly listed information. You can easily achieve that by replacing one-dimensional words with words that translate into emotions and visuals.

A. **Smell**

Many memories are recalled by just smelling a certain fragrance in the air. It can be the smell of a warm, home-cooked meal, a perfume someone close to your heart used to wear, the smell of fresh paint, or a freshly mowed lawn. The examples are literally endless. But the foundational fact here is that smell is one of the senses that serve in building a memory. In fact, it is the strongest linked to memory out of all the five senses. When you incorporate smell like a different dimension in your talk, you will succeed in evoking emotions and transporting your audience back and forward across time.

You can rely on your words to describe a smell through incorporating it in your story or while reciting a situation. For example, you can describe the smell of a room you once had an important meeting in by saying, "*I remember anxiously stepping into the room where I was about to have my first appraisal. I was met with a high end pervasive spicy aroma of the most intimidating executives in my company.*"

And of course, you can actually link your presentation to ascent by having an aroma diffuser around, but that's not the point here.

B. **Touch**

Touch is a great means of creating muscle memory. It works perfectly if you are demonstrating a product your audience can put their hands on. But it can be tricky when there is no room for demonstrations. It just might be irrelevant to your topic, or the number of people in the audience may be too high to do that. However, you don't need to have all your audience experience the impact of touch when you can ask only one or a couple of them to come up to you and describe how it feels to the rest. No matter what you aim to describe, always make sure that it relates to every single person in your audience. For example, we all remember how our favorite blanket felt, so you can use that as a description by saying, 'as snug as a blanket.' or 'as smooth as a baby's skin.'

C. **Taste**

This is perhaps the most difficult to physically demonstrate due to financial limitations and considering the numbers in your audience. But again, you can use your words to describe a feeling in relation to taste. For example, if you are talking about failures, you can say, "*Being fired brought a bitter taste to my mouth.*" Or if you're reciting a success story, you can use, "*Hearing the good news was as delicious as a freshly baked apple pie.*"

D. **Sight**

Here comes the impact of your visuals in full force. While it has been covered in detail in chapter 1, I'm going far beyond your choice of template. Show your audience something they haven't seen before, dig a little deeper to find images, which are not commonly used. You can always use pictures to contrast and compare. This is a technique commonly used by health advocates and nutritionists, where they usually showcase the prominent impact of adopting a healthy lifestyle on how a person looks. It's very much possible that you have encountered these techniques when used to convince people to drink more water, where the woman's face aged back after just 30 days, and the opposite when rallying against smoking (a woman face looks all wrinkly and old).

You can also follow that same line with charts. For example, if you're proposing a change in marketing strategy, you can show the stakeholders where they currently stand, and, after adopting your vision, where they will stand in terms of market share.

E. **Hearing**

The tone of your voice definitely sparks their sense of hearing, but while it's true that each one of us has a unique voiceprint, not everyone is gifted with selective listening skills. So, instead, you can take things to another level by mimicking the accent of someone you're referring to, or changing your voice to demonstrate the sound of someone else's voice. This is a very common technique used by comedians, where they help imprint the story even deeper, making it resonate on a deeper level through painting a complete mental image of the person they are roasting.

How can you communicate a compelling message in a concise manner?

There was an assessment tool some organizations used during the hiring process, where an executive would tell you, "You have 5 minutes to convince me to hire you."

You won't actually do that when presenting to an audience. After all, you have more than 5 minutes to deliver your speech, but it's the snappy edge that you can take away from the premise.

Think about it this way: If you have a very short time to communicate with anyone, what are the most important points you'd like to cover? And right there, you have your outline for the essential aspects, which you must absolutely state to make a case. Any additional points besides the ones you labeled as top priority are considered fluff. Don't dispose of them; keep them as additional information which you can use if you still have time or during post-presentation interaction. Then think of what comes before and after. In a way, it's as if you are dissecting your talk into three big chunks; the introduction, the core, and the conclusion.

1. **Eliminate the fluff**

There is no doubt that any topic is packed with endless heaps of information that you can include. But if you go down this road, you'll end up losing focus as well as your audience's attention. People hate sitting through repeated information as much as you do. Aim to provide fresh and uncommonly used data to spark their interest while remaining within the logical lanes of your topic. The best way is to revisit your through-line and decide what the core intent of your topic is and the reason why your audience would want to listen to it. As you outline the sequence of your presentation, prioritize the information at hand and start from there. Move down in a hierarchal manner from the most important to the least. Then begin to cross out all the added fluff until you strip your topic to the very core. Note that this won't happen in one sitting. You'd need to do it once, then step away and re-do the edits until you are comfortable with the content you end up with. Most of the time, it's the extra examples and stories that force the issue. Be selective when choosing the most relevant and impactful ones.

2. **Ditch the Bullets**

There are rules when it comes to using bullet points in your presentation. Remember the 2/4/8 rule we discussed in chapter 1?

However, you can stand out from the millions of presentations that rely heavily on bullet points and use prominent keywords instead. This way, your slides will look clean as you project a dark background with one word or two maximum while signaling what you are communicating in a lighter color. You can play along with that concept by using more slides, each with a single message, or one slide where one word appears once at a time. Using this technique can allow your audience to focus on the words you're saying rather than what you are showing. It also gives you more room to utilize nonverbal communication, which transfers to your audience a lot faster than reading alone.

You can also use this when relaying the most important message your audience should take away from your speech. Maybe have them complete a couple of sentences with the keywords you have been explaining throughout your presentation.

3. Use simple words that don't need further explanation

A key staple for delivering a concise presentation is the selection of words you employ. While it sounds sophisticated and can project you as the intellectual type, it can also give you away as someone who is distant and unreachable. Make things simple for you and your audience. Use words that are widely understood without any possibility of confusion. A trick that will definitely come in handy is thinking, "What if a 10-year-old were present among my audience - would they be able to follow what I'm saying?"

Replacing complicated words with simple ones can help you save up on all the extra minutes it would require for an explanation, and you will make way for other points you might wish to cover. But you have to consider the kind of audience you're addressing. As much as you don't want to sound too complex to the majority, you wouldn't want to come across as a beginner who lacks the foundational terminology of their topic.

4. Straight to the point

As much as it's important to eliminate the fluff from your presentation, it's crucial that you get to the point you want to communicate to your audience. You can follow the same line you would use when creating subtitles for a text; start by articulating the core point then move along with explanations or elaborations. But don't forget to assign reasonable minutes for each point, so you don't end up spending too much time on one at the expense of the other. A good way to do that is by creating a mind map for each 'subtitle' where you'll list 3 to 4 aspects you wish to cover for each. Also, it's important to remember that, while you're on stage narrating a story you are comfortable with, time tends to slip by without you even noticing. You don't want to lose your train of thought or break your audience's rhythm of attention by fixating on a certain part of your presentation for too long.

Chapter 7: You May be Nervous – It's Important not to Over-run your Time Slot

If you're anxious and dreading to present, feeling nauseous, and your palms are sweating, don't worry, you are not alone! There is a reason why 75% of the entire human race has admitted to the fear of public speaking. All presenters find it tough to perform sometimes.

This fear will definitely impact your confidence and, consequently, your overall performance, threatening your control over your rhythm. One of the major factors heavily impacted by panic is time control. Adhering to the given time frame is one of the successful elements of every presentation. Starting off, scared can make you rush into the presentation by talking too fast, thus failing drastically to grab your audience's attention. Or just aimlessly adding too much information because you are too afraid to overlook any point, which will only result in overloading your audience while failing to deliver your main message.

Either way, to help you avoid all of this, below is a detailed list of the most useful techniques that can help you curb your fears and diminish your worries.

First, let's fight the tension.

1. **Organizing your thoughts**

Before rehearsing your speech, list down all your thoughts and ideas on a piece of paper. Have them structured, until you reach clear headers you want to discuss. Getting things in place in an organized manner puts them in the right perspective, and accordingly will allow you to relax and stay calm. That's just an initial step to let you clear out the worries in your head and help you focus and think clearly.

2. **Prepare and Practice**

Learning a new skill, or taking on a different task, is always overwhelming at first. To reach a level of competency, in anything, you require to practice. And by that, we don't mean to practice once or twice, but as much as you need to achieve the necessary confidence and control over your content so you can get the job done right.

Rehearsing your presentation should be done more than once until you feel that you are comfortable and have a tight grip on the situation. Once you get there, a huge part of the tension will instantly melt away. As you gain control and fluency in your speech, you will get to a point where you don't even need to look at your material anymore. Instead, it will feel more like having a conversation where you'll get to share something you are really passionate about with a group of people.

3. **Pause and Breathe!**

Basically, you need to remember to breathe and practice it during the speech. Moderating your breathing with a composed tactic will convey a better echo to your voice, and eventually, calm you down. Laying it down in a scientific manner, breathing leads to enhanced blood circulation, which means more oxygen to the brain, and you'll become more alert. This, in turn, will help reduce the tension.

Also relevant to setting your breathing into a rhythm is catching a breath while talking. To achieve this, you need to learn to pause subtly without your audience noticing. If you are anxious, you might end up talking too fast, forcing you to breathe heavily towards the end of your lines. To avoid this from happening, work on your pauses, and practice when to stop and when to continue. Needless to say, this needs to be matched with your content. You do not want to suddenly stop in the middle of a statement, confusing your audience as to whether this is it or there is more to come.

Pausing and breathing are interrelated; you have to set your breathing rhythm and support this by knowing when to pause to fill up on oxygen.

4. **Workout or meditate**

Bringing home the importance of proper blood circulation for an adequate supply of oxygen to the brain leads us to stress the need for a well-rested and relaxed body.

If you have time on your hands, probably the day before your speech, it's highly advised to either meditate or get some light exercise in. You can go for a long walk to refresh and chill or do a few squats in the comfort of your home. This helps to promote the release of endorphins in the body, which in turn relieves pain and stress. The same applies when you meditate, as it clears your mind from any negative thoughts and again increases your blood circulation. You will be astonished by the tremendous effect of regular blood flow on your general well-being ahead of your presentation.

5. **Focus on your material, and not the audience's reactions**

While it's important to be audience-sensitive, sometimes people can throw you off with their grumpy facial expressions or sleepy body posture. Always remember that it's extremely hard to get a huge room full of people to agree on one thing; we are human beings with different inspirations and interests. So, keep an open mind to the idea that some of the attendees would be less attentive, not interested, yawning, or simply not paying attention. Accordingly, do not focus on the smaller bunch, making you nervous for no good reason. Instead, concentrate on your speech and delivery to serve the majority of the audience who actually want to listen.

6. **Hydrate well!**

A simple but highly required point to keep in mind is to be properly hydrated before doing all this talking. The last thing you need to worry about is feeling drowsy with a dry mouth. Drink moderate amounts of water ahead of your speech, but remember to hit the bathroom before going in!

Another good tip is having a cup of water with a squeeze of lemon before taking the stage. This mix acts as a good lubricant to the throat, avoiding any annoying dryness and glitches while talking. And, of course, if the presentation allows for it, have a bottle of water next to you during the talk.

7. **Exclude Fear of Rejection**

Refrain overthinking and plaguing yourself with negative thoughts, such as, *"What if they hate my presentation?"* or, *"What if they want me out of the room?"* This will get you nowhere and will only add to your fear. You were asked to speak because your hosts believe that you know what you're talking about. No one is setting you up for failure; only you can do that if you let your fear get the best of you. Instead, here are a few tricks to help you convert your anxiety to excitement.

It's very similar to the night before a very important exam, where you stay up all night studying, but instead of feeling ready, you get extremely tense and start to panic. On the other hand, the best performers in school usually adopt a different approach. Rather than sweating it and going over the material a hundred times, once they have practiced enough, they stop and enjoy something they love, or try to get energized in one way or another.

So it's highly recommended you do whatever it takes to feel enthusiastic, empowered, and eventually calm. Right before the presentation, here are a few options that might work for you; go watch a movie, listen to a certain type of music that makes you smile, or even gulp down an energy drink. Pick whatever suits you as an individual and go for it. Just create a new rule for yourself: When things get tough, you deserve to be pampered.

8. Arrive Early to adjust

It's always great advice to arrive at the venue earlier than needed, giving you plenty of time to settle in until you get acquainted with the place and learn how to navigate the equipment. If possible, make use of this time to check the room's amenities, such as lighting, the microphone, your perfect spot to walk around on stage to face the audience, and even any unexpected sounds that might be a source of distraction to you, such as loud and noisy traffic right outside the venue.

This is a great way to adapt comfortably since arriving late will make you tense and shatter all the effort done beforehand to push the fear aside.

It's important to note the fact that everyone is different. What might work for others doesn't necessarily have to work for you! You don't have to use only one of the aforementioned ways to calm your nerves. You can mix and match until you have established a routine you are comfortable with.

Now that this issue is put aside, it's time to focus on timing your delivery, so your audience gets to experience and enjoys all the material you've worked hard to gather and organize.

1. Determine your "Talking Time"

Most frequently, the organizers will provide a set time for your speech. Usually, the time allocated includes the actual presentation time in addition to the questions and answers part. So you should keep in mind that the "talking time" is not the total time provided. So, when preparing, be sure to do the following:

• You should ensure some time left for questions, and if it's your call, it's advisable to allow around 20% of the time provided.

• While rehearsing and timing your talk is an efficient tool, the actual live presentation usually takes up more time due to various external factors related to the place, people, or even equipment. So mind that by creating content, which will spare a couple of minutes.

2. Managing Content Delivery:

As always, it is encouraged in presentations to keep everything as concise as possible, but still delivering value that has a great impact on the audience and serves for easy recall. In that sense, let's take a stroll through a simple process that will allow you to deliver your content and keep it within the required time frame.

● Planning:

Start with writing an outline for your talk, and listing down the points to be covered in the proper logical order. For each point, brainstorm well to come up with the most concise and to the point statements, in order to explain and clarify what you need to say. Being able to focus on delivering short, powerful sentences will definitely free up some space for further and more innovative additions. For example, you can add value with some fascinating facts or supporting examples to impress. So plan it well to maximize the benefit.

● **Flexibility:**

Even if you go the extra mile and write an exact script of the whole presentation, it is still hard to memorize and will eventually be stressful to keep track of time spent trying to remember the exact words.

So listing down the main focus points as mentioned in the planning phase, along with thoroughly reading about your topic for further credibility and confidence, will leave you with a flexible smooth flow, which you can improvise on whenever needed to adapt for whatever changes easily or questions that may come your way.

3. **Time your Content**

Why is this crucial? Simply because we think a lot faster than we talk. So, if you keep repeating it in your head, you won't be able to tell how long it will take actually to say the words out loud. Using a stopwatch, limit each slide to an average of 45 seconds, and practice within this frame. This average takes into account the time you need when moving from one slide to another and provides enough gaps if any interruptions occur.

4. **Start Right on Time**

This is extremely crucial and can be a killer if missed. Start on time! Always! The last thing you need after all the effort exerted is to throw it all away by starting late! If everything is set in place and ready to go, simply do not wait for latecomers to start. Unless starting late is out of your hands, then you can always revert to the flexibility technique mentioned earlier in this chapter.

5. **Learn to adapt**

Despite all the preparations you have gone through up until this moment, unexpected situations may arise, throwing you off your planned and intended course. But remember, you have prepared a lot to be fully equipped with all the things you may need. Whether it's a technical issue, faulty room facilities, or anything else, don't sweat it. Relax and make the best out of the situation. The answer is not to hurdle and talk fast, but rather think ahead in regards to what can be compromised so that you still finish on time. For example, skipping on the least important section of your speech can make up for the time lost. But be careful that when you revert to such solutions, do not puzzle the audience by rushing through the slides just to reach the one you want. Try to transition to the intended destination smoothly, and be cool about it. This looks more professional and keeps the attendees focused without losing track of what you were just talking about.

6. **Don't get too attached**

Crafting any content from scratch entails a journey of thorough research, restructuring, and packaging the final material in an attractive form. During this time, you cherish every piece of information as you get to deeply think about the moment you are going to deliver it to your audience.

Some speakers tend to get too attached to their content that the mere idea of crossing out any one part causes them pain. Some refer to it as killing their own child. If you happen to be one of those speakers, there are always creative alternatives if you don't get the chance to present all the content you have prepared.

Post all the material you wish to share with your audience on your blog or website. That is, of course, if you don't mind public use of your material. But if you don't want open and free access to your content, you can provide your contact information so the audience can email you a request for your compiled material. And, of course, if you have the financial means, you can print out your content and have it distributed to your audience.

It's important to note that when you educate yourself about your topic and are prepared to the max, you reach the required confidence to present what needs to be delivered. So the next time anything comes your way, it won't be an issue. Just refrain from getting anxious at the first obstacle faced. Stop, take a second to breathe, and think, and you'll definitely come up with a variety of solutions relevant to the situation. At the end of the day, it all comes down to you!

Chapter 8: Any Questions?

We have all attended presentations where we start losing interest during wrap up. It feels like the energy has come to a halt, and there's nothing left to say, and unfortunately, all we can think of is when we can get out of there!

Many presenters aim to start their presentations keen to impress and grab their audience's attention but fail to do the same by the end of their talk.

Why does it just come to a buzz kill towards the end?

Because you start to lose the high note, thinking that you have already covered everything thoroughly, anxiously waiting for Q&A time. This is a big mistake! We're not saying that you should not take questions. On the contrary, you have to, but that should not be the end of it. As long as you are still on stage, maintain your star quality.

It's very crucial to highlight that the ending is as important as the introduction. This is where your audience either retains your content or loses a hefty chunk of it due to an uninspiring ending.

The following are some thought-provoking tricks and tips that can be used to create inspiring moments during closures.

1. Captivating Quotes

A lot of public speakers use quotes within their presentation or towards the end. But the trick lies in choosing the right ones rather than the frequently used and heavily worn-out quotes. In other words, look for new quotes mentioned by recent personalities. For example, a quote on marketing can originate from an up-to-date business person: *"Your culture is your brand,"* Tony Hsieh, CEO of <u>Zappos.com</u>.

It's not only about getting a unique and rarely listed quote, but you can also look for industry-specific quotes that are relevant to your clients or the organization you work for. Taking this approach usually makes a personal impact on the audience to which they will immensely relate to.

Another twist that will help in making this quote exclusive is adding to it yourself when relevant. In this case, it doesn't matter if you refer to a historical figure or not, because you are simply adding your unique touch. For example, *Heather Fleming, CEO of Catapult Design, once mentioned Gandhi's quote: "You have to be the change that you want to see in the world" but did not stop there and added the following lines: "But the part that was missing for me was getting the courage to be the change that you want to see in the world. I hope that we can all engage in that concept."*

With this kind of ending, you focus on one word in a quote and emphasize it to echo your final message. Moreover, it would be great to support this by properly visualizing it within your presentation slides. Maybe you can consider writing it in bold, powerful characters on a contrasting background that would instantly grab your audience's attention. For example, you can use white text on a black background, or add a splash of color by using a dark purple background and a white text.

TIP# 1: Quotes are a great way to use in your favor, elevating the impact of your work.

2. Amazing Fact

It can leave a great impact if you include realistic facts to spark your audience's imagination and challenge them enough to try and figure out how to apply this to their day-to-day life.

Take a look at the following example:

Venture capitalist Kevin O'Leary, during his speech at Global Entrepreneurship Week, discussed how to be a successful entrepreneur. Here, he decided to motivate his audience by using an astonishing fact instead of following the regular recapping method. He basically bombarded the audience with a tidbit about how there were more billion-dollar cap companies outside North America than in it. Needless to say, it had the desired effect on the crowd and really brought their attention back to his talk.

TIP#2: Use an astonishing fact to grasp the audience's attention and end on a high note.

3. Refer to your opening message

It's a frequent technique in wrapping up your speech to reinstate your opening statement. It could be done in more ways than one. For example, you might have popped a question at the start, so reverting back to the same question at the end would be a good time to answer it, and this reminds the audience of what the initial target was. Also, it can be a confirmation of your presentation title, referring to all that was covered and summing it up in a clear, yet creative way.

Reverting to the opening message doesn't only mean returning to a title, or a question asked earlier, but you can always go back to a story used during the introduction, which had an open-ended theme. Accordingly, using this method to recap frames the whole speech in a very organized manner, makes sure it's balanced and avoids any unanswered questions or misleading open-ended stories.

This technique is very similar to how stand-up comedians work on stage, where they regularly make jokes at the very beginning, and suddenly revisit those jokes at the end. This approach proves to be powerful when it generates a feeling of awareness and trust with the audience, making them feel like they have learned what they came for.

TIP#3: Use an open-ended story in the introduction and finish it at the end of your talk to end on a high note.

4. The Rule of 3

As modern science states, the human brain can capture a certain amount of information within a short time frame or what is referred to as 'active memory.' This basically means that the number of items we can easily remember is three to four pieces of information at a time. Hence, the rule of 3 was created.

After going through your entire content, you need to reemphasize your key messages. In order to achieve your goal, minimize them to 3 main points for a memorable, more enjoyable, and remarkable closure.

The rule of 3 is such an effective method that is easy to learn and practice, and can be applied to any industry or category of speech.

A few good examples are:

• Obama's Inaugural speech:

"Homes have been lost; jobs shed; businesses shuttered."

• Abraham Lincoln's Gettysburg Address:

"We cannot dedicate — we cannot consecrate — we cannot hallow — this ground." "Government of the people, by the people, for the people."

TIP#4: Minimize your key messages into three successive points to make it more memorable.

5. Persuasive Story

It's a very common closing technique, especially in educational and informative presentations. However, in cases like these, speakers present a 'case study,' which helps reinforce what had been covered without making it sound and feel relevant to their audience's lives.

However, if used properly, it can be used as an essential and powerful approach to creating empathy with the attendees, as it can help them relate to your topic on a deeper level rather than just receive the key messages from your speech as merely random information.

If you have already used a compelling story at the beginning and it has made its way to the audience's hearts, there's a huge chance it will deliver its magic at the end. This not only links them better with the topic but rather summarizes your speech in a creative and catchy manner that will be memorable for a long time.

TIP#5: Create or tell a real-life story that is commonly relevant to both the audience and your topic. It will help them connect and grasp their core messages.

6. **Thought-provoking question**

If you don't want to go with a story, or you can't find one that's relevant enough to add to your speech, don't worry. There are other ideas you can use.

Before summing up, lead on by introducing a challenging question. Ask your audience something that will stimulate them and keep them focused. A provocative question creates a positive, challenging vibe and shifts the audience from passive to active participants. Moderate your way through their answers and start picking the right words from one member of your audience and then move on to another to keep the flow going. Asking questions like these builds on your attendees' need to answer. It's human nature, especially if this question relates to their lives in one way or another.

This aids in reiterating the information shared during the presentation by having them translate it into their own, understandable way. This helps you maintain control of their attentiveness in an enjoyable way without boring them. Nevertheless, taking this approach helps you to achieve an interesting summary for the audience to remember.

TIP#6: It's crucial to bear in mind not to undermine or dismiss any of the answers. Instead, rephrase it in the right words whenever needed.

7. A Call to Action

Most business presentations, including those related to sales and marketing, are conducted with the intention to nudge the audience towards an action the presenter wants them to take. The best way to ensure that your message is loud and clear is by providing a strong call-to-action at the very end. Don't just assume that your message alone will encourage people to take action, but rather, point it out bluntly.

A call-to-action is influential in context but authoritative at the core, where you need to push forward and motivate your audience to ensure that they will follow and act accordingly. It's a powerful method that leads with a positive high note and eventually ends with an energetic tone.

You can follow this two-step approach to craft your call-to-action:

1. *Initiate with a negative scene: Although a bit dark, but projecting the worst will create a rejection of the status quo. Through employing such a scene, you will get to show them how badly things could go wrong if they do not proceed as suggested. There is a famous sales quote that says, "People don't buy their way into something, they buy their way out of a problem."*

2. *End with a positive scene: Showcase the positives of endorsement through projecting how things would be perfect if they pursue what you recommend.*

This technique is applicable in a wide variety of industries, such as sales, donations, marketing, even sports team meetings, and much more. So make use of it!

TIP#7: Craft your call-to-action in a compelling yet convincing manner.

8. Time-Sensitive messages

Each topic and message delivered requires to be put in the proper scope and magnitude of relevance. So, not only will you need to make impressive endings and a compelling call-to-action, but it is also important to frame each key point with the desired weight in terms of significance and required results.

It is very common among advertisers and marketers who need their clients to take action as soon as possible. These dynamic industries require an extremely high pace to keep up with market needs and competition. You can apply similar types of messages, usually referred to as "time-sensitive" messages, to urge or motivate your audience to go into action quickly.

Basically, it starts with the choice of words you use for your statement. They need to be powerful enough to engage, inspiring enough to motivate and be delivered quickly to put your audience on the track you want.

Another aspect is the tone used to motivate. It has to be on a high note, assertive, but not intimidating. So be careful, because it's a very thin line. You probably think that motivation in settings like these requires an extremely high and authoritative tone. But that's not how it works; you do not want your audience to feel like they are taking orders. On the contrary, you want them to feel motivated to endorse your call-to-action. The high pitched voice used needs to be illustrated with positive energy and sufficient encouragement.

Another fun part to add to your strategy is inserting a slide in your presentation with motion graphics. Make it a bold one, with clear and vivid visuals, adequately strong enough to make a statement.

TIP# 8: Use "time-sensitive" messages to motivate your audience to your call-to-action.

9. Powerful Visuals

You have definitely come across many articles that rave about the importance of sleek and professional slides, with the right use of colors depending on the mood, topic, and audience requirements. In this part, we'll be taking visuals to another level and specifically when ending your speech.

What we mean by visuals here are the pictures, portraits, paintings, etc., that have an instant effect, clearly, relate to your messages, and cultivates your main points as you move closer to wrapping up. It was once mentioned by theoretical physicist, Dr. Michio Kaku, that a huge part of the human brain is dedicated to processing pictorial imageries. Kaku says, *"It's how we communicate; it's how we share information, it's by images, pictures, videos that we understand the universe."*

TIP# 9: Turn a simple portrait into a sketched metaphor (there are many free apps that can do that for you), which instantly resides in the memory of your audience.

10. End with a Summary

It's time to end! You have answered all their inquiries and made sure everything was clear. Do not stop there! Hammer in your topic and relay your key points with a proper summary. Never leave the room without closure, or by just saying thank you when you are done with the slides.

This never leaves an impactful impression. You want to succeed and be remembered for your remarkable efforts, and you need to impress until the very end and relay your points in a simple yet to-the-point manner. Deliver your main points clearly, simply but thoroughly, in a way that recaps all that was said in just a few powerful words.

Leaving the room without a summary can result in the audience, forgetting most of what was covered. A human's concentration span differs among individuals. Accordingly, some of the attendees might have gotten lost at some point and did not have enough courage to ask a question.

TIP#10: Always close with a summary of your most important points to reinforce them.

11. Don't wrap up with Questions

This is a very common mistake within the public speaking domain. Be fully aware of these, especially towards closure. Why? Because just like the introduction, it can either be memorable, or it can tank while spreading negative feedback about you.

When starting the Q & A part of your presentation, you need to ensure you are extremely competent and prepared regarding the topic delivered. You never know what might come your way. An adverse question might end the day on a dismal note, which is something you wouldn't want considering the effort exerted in presenting and preparing.

TIP#11: Prepare a short closing statement after the Q&A phase is done, so you leave on a high note.

12. Make it crystal clear that you are done

Nothing is more disturbing than an awkward silence, especially when it occurs at the end of your speech. It makes the audience uncomfortable, as they are not sure whether it's time to go or if there's more to your presentation. This can kill the buzz of outstanding performance. It creates hesitance that immediately disrupts your audience's focus.

When ending your presentation, in whichever way you choose, make sure it's crystal clear that it's come to an end, and not just in an ambiguous silence followed by, "*That's about it, thank you.*" Your words need to portray that you're done obviously. Do that by employing a simple term like, "And finally," or "My final point is," or, "Today I want to leave you with..." In turn, the audience will instantly know that it is the end and, hopefully, react with a sign of appreciation.

TIP#12: Make sure to be as clear as possible that your talk is coming to an end. Do not ruin a good show with a single awkward moment.

13. Thank your Audience

Last but not least, thank you note. There is no doubt that you'd expect to be acknowledged with any form of thanks – I'm not talking about a standing ovation - but simple applause will do. After ending a presentation and exerting a lot of effort in initially preparing and then delivering, this completes your confidence and boosts your morale to present even more in the future.

But what about those active participants who have attentively listened and motivated you. Put yourself in their shoes. They definitely require some appreciation for their time and effort, as well. After all, they took time off their schedules just to listen and learn from you. So the least that could be offered is a simple thank you and salutation for their attendance and engagement. You have to be fully aware that your performance would have never been complete without their existence. So take a bit of your closure time and genuinely show your gratitude for their patience, support, and how you hope they will cross paths with you again.

Tip# 13: Thank you is a big deal. Don't forget that!

Chapter 9: Post Presentation

You would think that by wrapping up your talk and thanking the audience for listening that your job here is done. WRONG! There is still more time to connect with your audience, and I'm talking about the basic human interaction where you can get to know them, and they can get to know you as you step away from being the center of attention. Building a rapport like this, at this stage, holds a completely different meaning as it's now more about the audience than just passing along the knowledge. Your role shifts from just another speaker they've encountered to a friendly acquaintance and probably a trusted advisor.

Usually, people are curious to know more about someone they like, hence the tabloid business boom, and by achieving the likability status, you are setting yourself apart from any speaker they have ever witnessed. Moreover, people prefer to work with someone they are familiar with rather than a stranger, even if that person is not the best caliber for achieving a goal.

I know that sometimes, there is no room for you to interact with your audience after the presentation for various reasons. Maybe you have a commitment forcing you to leave immediately after the talk, maybe there is no Q&A slot allowed, and maybe it's your decision all along to finish and leave. But if there is a chance for you to stick around and mingle with people, do it! You will be surprised how much it will actually affect the audience's perception of you and the endless circle of new connections you can gain. After all, meeting a few new faces and building a network is always important.

If you want to gain a superior status and build an impactful connection with subtle finesse, but you have no clue how to achieve that, here are some of the most effective ways you can build rapport with your audience after presenting.

1. Shake hands and give a welcoming smile

I know that at this point, you are exhausted, and all you can think of is the hearty meal you wish to devour, but as someone from your audience walks up to you for further inquiries or comments, always welcome them with an inviting, warm smile. A strong shake of the hand would draw out the first spark that you are open and interested in whatever it is they are about to tell you. It is advisable that you lead every conversation subtly, simply by asking for their name, their background, and the reason for attending your talk. In an indirect way, you'd be surveying your audience and gathering up information that you can use as a future reference for what it is that they wish to leave with.

2. Use casual language

Being on stage imposes a level of formality on the selection of wordings you use. Regardless of the nature of the talk, you are constantly aware that you have to come across as the expert, someone who is experienced, and has something to add to the audience's knowledge, or else you wouldn't be the one chosen to give the speech. You are also meticulous when it comes to choosing jokes and the context as a whole in order to avoid offending anyone. But when it is time to have a private conversation with your attendees, you must level with them through letting your guard down and speaking from the heart. For this to happen, adjust your conversation to their own terminologies. You are on their turf now, so grab what they give you and construct your response using their own words. For example, if they refer to your business as a 'service,' you too should refer to it as a service. If you are addressing a gender issue while they call it women's issues, then you should refer to it the same way as well. This brings a whole new level of closeness to the discussion, signaling a magnitude of relevance that goes both ways.

3. Share your story

If you haven't done so already while on stage, it would serve you best to talk about your life experiences when engaging in a conversation with one or more of the members of your audience. You will come across as someone who is reachable and relevant. For example, if they come up to you to share their story of how they got started in entrepreneurship, you can use that to secure rapport through sharing your own version of how you got started. Or if they tackle a certain hardship they faced in life or their career; you probably have a relevant story to share about yourself or someone you know. It's important not to limit your response to a compassionate nod or brief words that fall in line with "I know" or "that's unfair" or "good for you." However, don't be too overwhelming. You need to share, but you don't need to overshare to the extent of silencing them where there is no space for them to talk.

4. Networking without pitching

That's just another mistake many presenters fall into as they try to mingle with their audience. No matter how many business cards you give out or the targeted number of cards you wish to collect, post-presentation is not a convenient time to propose a business venture. It is all about networking and getting to know the people better. The moment you stepped on the stage, they've crafted their first impression of you, and while presenting, this perception either changed or was reassured, and now you are closing with the right impression you wish for them to leave with of you. Even if someone comes up to you with a tempting offer or another potential chance for you to present at a different venue, express your interest to join but set up a meeting in a more formal setting to discuss further details.

5. **Build on your efforts**

Post collecting the contact details of all the new people you've met on presentation day, it's time to lock in the connection. Usually, there is a maximum time span allowed for contacting someone you've recently encountered, and that is up to 48 hours. It's the appropriate amount of time when your memory is still freshly carved in their minds. Make the best use of social networking tools such as LinkedIn, Instagram, and Facebook, and you can always drop in an email if that's how they prefer to be contacted. Keep the approach friendly by introducing yourself, where you had met, and what had been discussed. Emphasize how happy you were by the encounter and that you look forward to future meetings. And always remember to avoid proposing anything, whether it's a business deal or future endeavors. However, if that was your initial aim for the contact and it was what your correspondent is waiting for, then request a meeting referring to what you wish to discuss with them.

6. **Walk up to people**

There is a slim chance that no one would walk up to you after the presentation, but if you are the introvert type and it just so happens that you walk into a room full of people who are busy chatting, take the first step. Make it a goal to talk to a certain number of people; the goal shouldn't be sky-high, a range from 5 to 8 is an excellent start. Walk up to someone from the audience you have noticed and ask for their feedback, but mind the way in which you speak, as you don't want to give them mixed signals. Seek an organizer or a fellow speaker and initiate a conversation. It's like the saying goes, "Don't go unnoticed," and that should be your aim. Minutes ago, you were on stage, and now it's time for you to get to know the people with whom you've shared a room. Use this opportunity to get some comments or remarks and break the cycle of standing alone, scared in the corner.

Reflecting Back

After the day is done, it's important to reflect back on what happened. Like rewinding a tape with all its details from the moment you've learned about being assigned to give that presentation to how you managed your time during preparation and on stage, to the techniques and tools you adopted for delivery. All of the aforementioned aspects need to be revisited in order to advance and develop your skills in a more prosperous light.

That being said, there is a simple technique to use when assessing any presentation. It's through dividing the whole experience into a pros and cons format while using the negatives to establish an action plan for how this can be improved. It's all about being realistic; you don't want to be an extreme on either side, just the plain truth. Of course, it would help immensely if your live presentation was videotaped so you can not only asses the pace and the content, but the way you looked to the audience, your voice tone, and general body language.

Now let's begin!

So, what went well?

There is no doubt that there are many aspects of your presentation where you deserve a pat on the back. And knowing that this might be an overwhelming phase, there is an easier way you can review your performance. Focus on the main elements, which can make or break any presentation. You can use the aspects we have covered so far as an indication. Or you can ask yourself the following ten questions:

- *How did it feel going on stage? Is it something that I would want to do again?*

- *What was the highest point of my speech? - The introduction, the core context, at the end?*

- *When did I start to relax and easily glide through the presentation?*

- *From the various tools I used, which clicked the most with the audience?*

- *Was I able to cover all of the points I wanted to address?*

- *Did I manage my time well on stage?*

- *Did the audience seem interested and engaged?*

- *Was the audience focused and interactive?*

- *When did I feel like I was losing them?*

And finally, ask yourself, "**What could I have done better?**"

You need to be super honest with yourself. You have to put aside all of the positive feedback that is packed with encouraging words, the congratulatory phrases, and the well-expressed gratitude from your audience because you are your toughest critic. Only you know what you are capable of and what you could have done better. It doesn't necessarily mean that you should only look at the drawbacks. Sometimes the presentation truly does go perfectly well. But all we're saying is that you were on your own, hoarding the hours researching, drafting, scripting, and practicing, and only you can define the areas where there is room for improvement when it comes to your presentation skills.

Before we tap into that, there is one thing you need to avoid in order to move towards being a better public speaker; that dark Post Presentation Anxiety, mostly known Post Party Syndrome (PPS). As the dust begins to settle, and all the allure from the audience's positive feedback starts to fade, a cloud of doubt begins to circle your mind. You start to recall all the core messages you could have communicated better, the additional examples you could have added to explain a point further, and the many relatable stories you could have shared.

This notion of self-doubt could be crippling, especially if the talk went really well. Some experts prefer to throw all the PPS effects out the window and look at the brighter side, which is being invited to speak in the first place or being selected to conduct that business presentation. But, yet again, people learn from their experiences as well as their mistakes, and you should never let that go without harvesting the benefits. Thus, the adjustments should be actionable. Just like grading papers, you need to give feedback, but at the same time, provide the students with the guidelines they would need to follow for the assignment to be granted a higher grade. In other words, your plan must translate into what you can do about the presentation elements that you are not satisfied with. How can you improve them? What new skills do you need to develop? What other ideas can you use to deliver your message in a clearer sense?

Allow us to demonstrate.

First, start by listing all areas of concern, the areas you know you could have done a better job at, regardless of what the audience thought. Then, follow each point with what you believe could make the problem go away or enhance the outcome.

Areas of concern

Ways to Improve

I feel I sounded boring.

• Only talk about issues you are passionate about or try to get invested in the topic through finding points of interest.

- Sign up for a voice coaching class to learn how to play with your tone to captivate your audience, emphasize a point, and channel emotions.

- Listen to other presenters and take notes on how they manage to convey a message in an interesting manner.

- Research ideas to keep the audience interested.

I didn't know what to do with my hands.

- Watch videos by other presenters and take notes on how they use their body language.

- Watch videos on how to incorporate body language in a presentation.

- Research the different indications for each body language.

- Practice what you have learned in your day-to-day life.

I lost focus and had to repeat a couple of points.

- Map out the content of the presentation.

- Memorize the content through visuals.

- Use different colors on your note cards, indicating an example, a story, or statistic.

- Practice with distractions.

I felt my argument wasn't compelling enough.

• Learn about persuasive communication.

• Research negotiation skills.

• Sign up for a sales course.

• Gather more data for your next topic that addresses the Ethos, Pathos, and Logos elements of persuasion.

Chapter 10: How Can I Put Things Right When they go Wrong?

Giving a presentation, while an enjoyable experience, can be stressful on its own, let alone having to worry about all the things that can fail while on stage. The tricky part here is that there is no room to hide, given the fact that you are performing live in front of the audience you wish to impact.

During these tough times, you'll experience another level of anxiousness, which can reflect badly on your status as a professional speaker. That's why lots of professional speakers tend to do without technology altogether to save up on the additional hassle. But that doesn't mean you should too! My approach is always, why avoid it if it adds more to the depth and value of your presentation, especially if you can fix it? It all has to do with the way you perceive things that go wrong; is it an obstacle or a lesson well learned for improvement?

It's ok to experience one or more presentations where you were not at the top of your game. It happens to everyone. Even the best of the best speakers have come face to face with a delivery they weren't satisfied with, or their audience hasn't received well. The important thing is to learn the reasons why your presentation tanked, recover, take the necessary precautions to prevent it from happening again, and move on onto the next.

And don't ever think your efforts would go unnoticed by the audience. Trust me; everyone has witnessed their fair share of presentations, even if only online, to tell the difference between the speaker who stumbled on stage and another who stacked up the hours to deliver big moments.

When you go the extra mile in preparing your content, it shows. When you work extra hours on the theme and design of your slides, it shows. Even when things look like they're falling apart, the way you handle them will project a positive image of you as a professional speaker who allows nothing to get in their way.

This chapter will serve as a compiling guide that you can refer to with ease, for everything that can go wrong during a presentation and the ways you can turn events around to make them work in your favor.

1. Visuals Disasters

PowerPoint is a visual tool, not a script. But sometimes you can get carried away with the number of slides or the number of words each slide contains. Either way, it's bound to drive your presentation to a halt. Between a distracted audience and you feeling overwhelmed lies the elephant in the room: Your PowerPoint had sucked the rhythm out of your speech. That doesn't necessarily have to happen to you, especially after you have gone through chapter 1, but believe it or not, it does happen to those who keep the slides clean without minding their count or vice versa. There are two more ways your data show can be a disappointment, which is having empty space than words per slide, and substituting visuals for words. All of the aforementioned mishaps can be fixed if you are still relaxed in the comfort of your home. But what if that happens while you're presenting? When you realize that your slides look dull when magnified by a projector?

So how can you make things right?

• You can always revert to the main slide of your presentation to serve as the main backdrop while you are addressing the points you wish to cover.

• Communicate with your audience that you will provide the slides as a handout for them to take away from the organizers. Or, if you are presenting to a small number of people, ask for their emails to send them the material afterward.

• Apologize for the mistake and pretend that a swap had happened where the old draft was used instead of the final version.

- Maximize the images and ditch the words, improvising with the description and explanation. But, of course, remain loyal to the outline you have crafted.

2. Nonverbal Mishaps

Our nonverbal communication skills are acquired by habit and shaped by our close circle of friends and family. More often than not, you can find yourself waving your hands a lot or fidgeting as you speak. At other times you might catch yourself using the wrong body language that does not match what you're saying. For example, notice if, when you are expressing gratitude, you are shaking your head from left to right instead of up and down. These incorrect combinations would negate the meaning of your words and reinforce what your body language is saying. It's a situation similar to when someone is asking you if you've got the time to listen; while you might respond with a 'yes,' your body might be facing the direction of the exit. Again, a definite sign that you don't have the time to spare.

Moreover, people usually use high paced and pitched tones to express excitement or anger, while a slower pace and lower pitch signals, comfort, confidence, or fear. If you do otherwise, your words will lose their meaning. The same effect channels from monotonous people who lack 'color' in their voice. Those may be a part of what makes you … you! But when presenting, those are the exact elements of your day-to-day attitude that you need to completely and utterly ditch. Why? Simply because they crush your intended message, confuse your audience, or even worse, force them into a sleeping mode.

So how can you make things right?

• Rehearse your presentation in front of a mirror to fix incorrect body language.

• Record your speech to detect the redundancies in your voice and the areas you need to highlight with your tone.

• Make sure to familiarize yourself with the content of your presentation to focus on projecting the right nonverbal signs.

• Practice in your everyday life the new nonverbal skills you'd like to embrace while talking to people.

3. Not prepared enough!

There is nothing more annoying than wasting time listening to someone who 'acts' like they know what they're talking about, when the truth is, they don't know much at all. It's considered the sin of procrastination. Never jeopardize your credibility for anything. If you don't know the topic, either learn about it or reject the idea of presenting until you're ready. You might think that your audience won't notice this mishap, but you'd be surprised at how easily they can pick up on that. Throughout your career, you might forget that encounter, but the impression your audience makes of you will last for a long time, and it will take even longer to change it.

That is, of course, if you get the chance to present to them again.

So how can you make things right?

• Always and forever stick to what you know and elaborate on just that.

• Don't improvise, so you don't end up looking like a hoax.

• When asked a question, you absolutely have no proper answer for, state that clearly, and gives them a promise to read more about it.

4. Crippled by fear

When coaching a client once, she clearly understood everything taught to her, theoretically. But once asked to stand in the middle of the room to practice what she had been taught, something very strange happened. Although no one was present in the room, she started to shake visibly and sweat profusely. She had never presented before, but currently, it was part of her job. It took more than a couple of sessions to calm her down and reinstate her self-confidence.

You might not experience such extremes, but sometimes glossophobia (fear of public speaking) hits when you least expect it. Most experienced speakers would tell you that the hardest parts to get over are the few moments before they are going to take the stage and the first few minutes of your talk, after which you'll begin to loosen up as you get used to the surrounding.

So how can you make things right?

• Turn it to your advantage by knowing the parts you're most anxious about and working harder at that.

• Practice as many times as you need until there is no room for further alterations. Now you are confident that you know every aspect of your presentation by heart.

• Visualize your success in delivering your content with passion and finesse.

Embrace the fear as a normal reaction to someone who cares about what they do has.

• Establish a comfortable routine before presenting, like listening to music, meditation, or going for a run.

5. Annoying Repetitions.

Repeating a lot of "Umm's" and "uhh's" while speaking is a sign of lack of communication eloquence. One of the worst things is having to sit through a presentation with a speaker who stutters so much that it's almost predictable when he will utter the next interjection. This happens when you're either experiencing stage fright or trying to gather your thoughts to move to the following point. We all know that it often happens subconsciously, but it needs to stop once and for all! Frequent repetitions threaten your credibility as a speaker as it translates into your inability to communicate effectively.

So how can you make things right?

• Practice out loud. Most people who face this problem don't experience repetitions unless they can hear their voice out loud.

• Practice in front of people to overcome the fear of speaking in public.

• Increase your memory span through various brain exercises such as downloading a memory card game app or writing down a grocery list. Memorize it, and after an hour, recite what you remember. Repeat until you cross out all the items on your list.

6. Overrun the time

Exceeding the time allowed for your talk is one of the most common mistakes lots of speakers fall into. Between losing your train of thought, getting caught up in sharing a story, reacting to audience comments, and amplifying a focal point over the other, there are lots of things that can take up time. Of course, not to mention any technical problems that may arise and require a bit of stalling. It is quite the embarrassment if you have to be reminded by an audience member or one of the organizers that your time is up, and you should vacate for the following speaker. Or worse, that your audience, be it the general audience or stakeholders, have other things to tend to. Sometimes you can get crammed in time due to a previous speaker who has overrun their time.

So how can you make things right?

• First, aim to prioritize your content to present the most important points first and keep the least important at the end.

• Second, practice your speech with a stopwatch to time it perfectly and take notes of the areas where you tend to dwell on.

• Third, bear in mind that when performing live, your speech may run a little longer for any of the aforementioned reasons.

• And finally, go over your content, strike out all the unnecessary points, and place them on the side as extra notes or additional information that you can revisit if you need to.

7. Losing your train of thought

As the common saying goes, it comes with the territory. The more you get anxious about the presentation, and the higher you build up your expectations, the more you'll pressure yourself. And that is a disaster in disguise, for you'll end up lost with every little distraction, and your mind will just wander. Another reason you will feel lost is relying on memorizing. The problem here is that if one word slips your mind, the whole thing can come crashing down around you. The best method is to familiarize yourself with the content and sequence of your presentation. You can achieve this by constantly practicing the outline of your presentation (this is the part that you can memorize) and just read the rest of the content, thus avoiding the recitation word for word.

So how can you make things right?

• Practice! Practice! Practice!

• Create a mind map where you can link the focal points of your presentation in a linear way, using colors and shapes that seem logical to you. So, even if you go blank for a moment, you can instantly visualize the map and pick up right where you left off.

• Practice the 20/20/20 rule! According to memory experts, going over your presentation for 20 minutes, then repeat the entire sequence of your content twice can help. One stipulation is that if you don't repeat for the third time within a span of 20 minutes, parts of your material will literally be forgotten.

• Make it seem casual as if it were an intentional pause. You can grab a cup of water or move across the stage until you gather your thoughts.

• Although we advise against this method since it's preferable to avoid anything that can jeopardize your status as a professional speaker, if all else fails, you can ask the audience where you left off.

• Another technique that is generally frowned upon is to joke about it openly. For instance, saying, "Wow! I think I'm growing old here! What was I saying?"

8. A heckler among the crowd

The world is filled with as many haters as supporters. That's just a fact of life! And at some point, you will cross paths with an audience member who wants to challenge you, steal the show, or stir up chaos. In times like these, your primary focus should be on controlling your temper and maintaining your poise. Nothing can add salt to the wound, like escalating an already tough situation. Your second thought should focus on what to do to avert the attention away from that heckler and regain the rhythm of your presentation.

So how can you make things right?

• After welcoming your audience, it's better to lay down some ground rules on how you would like to moderate the talk. Speak with a hint of assertiveness if it's your plan to postpone any questions or comments until after you're done.

• Don't accept any interruptions, regardless of what the reason may be. Instead, politely say, "Can we please keep all questions at the end?" while generally looking at the crowd.

• If this person persists in talking, try to ignore them and move on with your presentation.

- Try to mask your frustration by using a joke or commenting sarcastically, "It's that urgent, huh? I can give you my contacts after the presentation, and we can argue all night if you want."

- Don't provoke the audience by offending any of them, even if they too are annoyed by the interruption.

- If he/she doesn't stop, you can ask that they are escorted out to carry on with the talk.

9. Technological fails

It's an inevitable nightmare that no one seems to escape! At some point, in one of your presentations, technology will turn its back on you. It's either that or the organizers can just forget your prerequisite list of equipment and/or software you need, or of course, the incompatibility warning sign that pops on the screen more often than none.

So how can you make things right?

- As you prepare for the presentation, aim to rehearse a couple of times without the slides as a background effect. You can still have them around to guide you, in print, but in worst-case scenarios, only you will get to see them.

- Prepare an alternative plan for when PowerPoint won't come up on the screen. Think about other attention-grabbing techniques you can use to entice your audience without the visual effects. (Refer back to chapter 2 for plan B ideas).

• If there is no technician available on the premises to fix what has suddenly halted, don't attempt to fix it yourself. Remember, you're on a time crunch, and you need every minute to deliver your content in a relaxed and seamless manner.

• If the problem arises with the clicker, you can ask one of the audience members to be "your assistant for the day" or what professors like to call a "mini-me" to manually change your slides in case the computer is not in reach.

• If the issue has to do with the microphone, well, that depends on the size of the venue. Sometimes it's a good idea to move around the audience or raise your voice. In most cases, you will need to stall a bit until the organizers provide you with another one.

10. Audience loses Interest

When the topic of your presentation is heavy, it's always advisable to address the issue in a vertical manner rather than a horizontal one. In a simpler sense, instead of trying to cover all aspects of your topic and anything that is remotely related to it, attempt to select 3 to 4 main subtitles and go deep into those.

Other times it's just the length of your talk that can force your audience to lose interest. Remember that this is normal, where after approximately 20 min through your presentation, your audience will draw back into their own thoughts.

So how can you make things right?

• Break the rhythm of your presentation with a visual you can build on. Remember the "breaker slide"?

• Engage your audience in an activity they can do instead of sitting down passively and listening to you as you speak.

• If possible, move them around, ask them to switch places, or invite them to do a quick stretch.

• Use humor to bring their attention back through a sarcastic comment or a joke.

• Use a provocative unclear image and ask them to think of how this is related to your topic.

And Finally

Presenting means that you have something to say that is deemed valuable for sharing, so make it worth your audience's while. Make your best effort to communicate an impactful speech, and don't forget to enjoy the experience! Giving a presentation is an honor, not a chore. Through presenting, you are sharing knowledge, and it's a form of art that keeps on giving. It will enrich you as much as it will add to your audience.

Conclusion

While it's true that there are no strict rules for presenting, there are some fundamental elements that, if utilized and executed perfectly, can change the impact of any talk on an audience. These elements can be categorized under three groups; the content, the assisting aids (visuals), and the delivery. But as you have probably noticed, while reading this book, these three groups are interchangeable. They can be shuffled among each phase, from preparing for the presentation to rehearsing, to taking the stage, to post-presentation interactions.

With each phase, one element can overshadow the other. For example, while preparing for your speech, your content plays the lead role, demanding all your attention as you gather and organize the data relevant to your topic. And it doesn't matter whether you decide to use a slide show or not, as many great speakers can still give compelling presentations without one. On the other hand, as you take the stage, your delivery, which includes your presence, the words you choose to use, your body language and voice tone become the focal point of the presentation.

Although the way you use each element might change as you move forward from sitting behind your desk to leaving the venue, the main purpose doesn't vary. In other words, the content provides the value your audience is eager to gain; the visuals communicate your message in a clearer light, and your delivery is the coloring you can employ to bring life to your message. None of these can substitute the other, or else it wouldn't be called a "presentation," but rather transforms into listening to an audiobook. Therefore, it all comes down to how you use these tools to produce the effect you desire on your audience.

Acquiring presentation skills needs time to develop and enhance. Remember, it's a skill after all, which means that if it's not practiced frequently, it can slowly become tarnished and die. Think of it as a work in progress, but in this case, the progress never ends. Just like we, as human beings, live and learn constantly, presentation skills are no exception. Simply because the audience's nature and the purpose behind any speech are not constant. Nothing is set in stone here! It doesn't matter how many times you're presenting the same topic if the audience demographic is regularly changing and vice versa. Any professional speaker, professor, or teacher can tell you that. Regardless of how many times they're addressing the very same topic or giving the same lecture or lesson, their delivery techniques and reliance on visual aids definitely change. So it all boils down to how you truly know your tools and audience to cater to your presentation according to their needs.

There are a couple of things you need to keep in mind as you present any topic, but it's mainly how you start that matters. Remember that your message has to be crystal clear before it is presented to the audience. You need to know how to describe what your topic is about with ease so it can serve you while you outline your speech and your slides. And given the fact that presenting relies heavily on performance that sets the tone for how much you put in your slides versus how much you articulate and express. This also limits your audience's distractions, as they tend to deviate their attention to reading rather than listening.

As with everything in life, presentations have a time span, which restricts your content to an annoying extent and compels you to deliver in a straight-to-the-point and simple approach. But concise doesn't mean weak; you can still cover a lot of points with the mere use of an image or narrating an emotionally packed story. Another important pitfall to bear in mind is how unreliable technology can be at times. While it can add another attention-grabbing dimension to your presentation, it can cripple your plans if it fails. Thus, have a plan B safely stashed for a rainy day.

What this book aims to provide is a detailed autopsy of every minute portion you are going to face as you embark on this exciting journey of giving a presentation. It presents a step-by-step guide packed with real-life examples and applicable alternatives that you can use when worse comes to worst. It also backs a call-to-action as you get to identify your weakest points, which you need to embellish for productive use in the future. In addition to that, you also have quick checklists that you can easily make use of to ensure that you've gotten all the elements of your speech covered.

Throughout this book, we presented you with lots of ideas and examples for the most critical two high points of your speech, which are the introduction and the closing. To achieve that, the chapters tapped into different disciplines, like rhetoric and emotional intelligence, to gather up the most effective tricks you can adopt to deliver an impactful and persuasive presentation.

And here's a piece of advice that we want to leave you with: Our all-time favorite 3C's to accompany you whenever you are scheduled to give a presentation.

Be Confident! In your knowledge through reading and reading even more about your topic … In you as a distinguished caliber … In your skills that you have worked hard to develop and improve … In your passion that it is worthy of people's time … In knowing that every mistake is a lesson learned… In your journey that got you to where you are today and shall guide you to higher places and achievements.

Be comfortable! With your own unique presence … With the attire, you choose to wear … With how much you stand out amongst the crowd … With your anxiousness, knowing that it will fuel your success … With being surrounded by people … With knowing that anything that can go wrong, you can make right.

Be creative! With your words … With your visuals … With the way, you tell a story … With getting to know your audience … With ways to grab their attention … With the details of your topic … Creating your signature presentation style.

Now go out there and shine!

Printed in Great Britain
by Amazon

81006260R00082